A Short Guide to Classical Mythology

A Short Guide to
Classical Mythology

G.M. Kirkwood
Cornell University

Bolchazy-Carducci Publishers, Inc.
Mundelein, Illinois USA

Cover Design: Adam Phillip Velez

A Short Guide to Classical Mythology

G.M. Kirkwood

2003, 2000 Reprint with correction of the
1959 Holt, Rinehart and Winston edition

Bolchazy-Carducci Publishers, Inc.
1570 Baskin Road
Mundelein, Illinois 60060
www.bolchazy.com

Printed in the United States of America
2017
by United Graphics

ISBN 978-0-86516-309-6

Library of Congress Cataloging-in-Publication Data

Kirkwood, Gordon MacDonald, 1916–
    A short guide to classical mythology / G.M. Kirkwood
        p. cm.
    Originally published: Fort Worth : Holt, Rinehart and Winston, 1959
    Includes bibliograpical references.
    ISBN 0-86516-309-X (pbk. : alk. paper)
    1. Mythology, Greek--Dictionaries.   I. Title.
    BL782.K58 1995
    292.1'3'03--dc20

                                                            95–43579
                                                                CIP

HOW TO READ THIS BOOK

Mythology has many aspects and many uses, and a guide to classical mythology might serve one or more of several purposes. It might stress the religious significance of the myths, or present them in the light of their meaning for Greek and Roman history, or analyze them from the point of view of anthropology or psychology. Or it might treat them, as they are treated in this book, essentially as stories, emphasizing their importance in literature. Whatever else a myth may be, it is a story, and the Greek word *mythos* means just that, "story." No doubt the ancestors of many of these stories were once upon a time told to explain the phenomena that surrounded and puzzled the teller and his audience, or to authenticate customs and beliefs. But the one sure and consistent fact about the Greek myths is that they are, as they have come to us, lively and satisfying stories, and it is this that makes them continue, in age after age, to be a quarry for poets and a delight for readers.

In this book the selection and treatment of myths are, then, influenced by their importance in ancient and modern literature. (A few myths are included which are negligible in literature, the story of Melampus, for example. In this instance and some others, the intrinsic interest of the myth justifies its inclusion.) To aid the process of selection, the mythological references of a number of important English poets (Chaucer, Spenser, Shakespeare, Jonson, Milton, Dryden, Wordsworth, Byron, Keats, Shelley, Tennyson, Landor, Arnold, Browning, Swinburne, and Eliot) were compiled and used as a guide. An effort has been made to render the book useful also for the most commonly read classics of other European literatures: the Greek tragedies, for example, and the *Divine Comedy*. Completeness could not be attempted, but it is thought that no myths that have been conspicuously or repeatedly used in literature have been omitted.

A short book that tries to cover as much ground as this one must be compressed. It is hoped that by having many short entries, with a few long and comprehensive entries, two aims will be served: to provide a reasonably complete reference list for the student of literature, and to convey the principal stories of classical mythology in a way that does not wholly rob them of their quality as stories. Reference is made from one entry to another by printing in bold type, within the body of the text, the word (usually a name) for which the reader is to consult another entry. Reference is made only when some information about the person or thing concerned is to be found in the entry referred to; thus the Trojan War does not appear in the form **Trojan War** every time it is mentioned, but only when the topic of discussion is further discussed in the entry **Trojan War.**

A few of the longest entries have been divided into sections introduced by italicized headings, as an aid in finding references. Thus, for example, the long entry on the Argonauts has sections headed *Background, Outward voyage, Colchis, Return voyage,* and *Corinth,* and the entry on Aeetes refers the reader to **Argonauts** (*Colchis*). Explicit references to sections are not given when there is some other indication of what section of the long entry is to be consulted. The short entries are mere reminders or identifications. When detailed information is provided it is in the long entry or entries to which a reference is given.

Two further remarks about the scope of this book remain to be made. The story of Pyramus and Thisbe is not really a myth but a *novella,* a brief romantic tale. It is, however, so familiar and so closely associated with classical myths because of its presence in Ovid's *Metamorphoses* that it had to be included. Other *novelle,* such as the story of Iphis and Anaxarete, which have by their nature as much right to inclusion but are less familiar, have been omitted. The term "classical" rather than "Greek" mythology may seem unjustified, because the Roman stories are few and unfamiliar (such as the stories of Picus and Vertumnus), and the one great Roman story, that of Aeneas, is partly Greek in origin. Nevertheless, these myths, as they have come to us, are a heritage of Rome as well as of Greece. The stories are Greek, to be sure; but their transmission to us, and hence their literary form and spirit, are often due to Latin poetry. No one would argue that the *Library* of Apollodorus, the most complete of our Greek source books of
* myth, is as important or influential as the *Metamorphoses.* In fact, only within the past century have writers in English commonly used the Greek names of the Greek gods and heroes; formerly, if a Roman name existed, it was the one customarily used, even when the story was taken directly from a Greek source. Shelley, in *Prometheus Unbound,* speaks of Jupiter, not Zeus, and Hercules, not Heracles. This book follows the current practice of using the Greek names. Roman names are used only in Roman stories, though of course the Roman names are listed in their alphabetical places, and reference is there made to the entry under the corresponding Greek name.

With regard to spelling, the traditional way, and the closest there is to a standard system, is to use Latinized spellings of Greek names. Many poets and translators nowadays try to keep certain elements of the Greek spellings, but nothing like a consistent usage has been evolved. There has, not surprisingly, been a retreat from such adventurousness as that of Browning; it is unlikely that anyone now would write, as he did, "Kuklops" for "Cyclops." The only difficulty that is likely to arise concerns *c* and *k;* the reader will have to look under *c* in this book for names that are sometimes spelled with an initial *k.* The chief differences between Latinized and Greek spellings are

> *c* for *k* (kappa): e.g., "Cassandra" for "Kassandra."
>
> *y* for *u* (upsilon), except in diphthongs: "Calypso" for "Kalupso," but "Atreus" retains *u.*
>
> *-us* for *-os* in noun endings when the *o* is short (omicron): "Patroclus" for "Patroklos." But long *o* (omega) is unchanged, as in "Minos." Short *o* is

*read: Ovid, *Metamorphoses*

sometimes kept in noun endings, especially in the names of islands, as "Delos." ("Cos," however, has long *o*.)

ae for *ai*: "Aegisthus" for "Aigisthos."

i or *e* for *ei*: "Iphigenia" for "Iphigeneia"; "Medea" for "Medeia." But *ei* is sometimes kept, as in "Poseidon."

oe for *oi*: "Phoenix" for "Phoinix." But *oi* is sometimes kept, as in "Moirae."

i for *oi* in word endings: "Delphi" for "Delphoi."

u for *ou*: "Oedipus" for "Oidipous."

The indications of pronunciation that are given in parentheses follow a simple system. A slanting stroke follows the part of the word to be accented, as "Ajax" (ā′jaks). Vowel sounds marked *ā, ē, ī, ō*, and *ū* are pronounced as English "long" vowels: f*a*te, sc*e*ne, r*i*de, r*o*de, and c*u*re, respectively. Note particularly that the sound marked *ū*, as in "Atreus" (ā′trūs), is pronounced like the *u* in "cure." When the sound of *u* in "prune" is called for, it is indicated by *ōō*, as in "Pluto" (plōō′tō). The sound of *e* as in "peril" is indicated by *ĕ* to distinguish it from the sound of *e* as in "fern," which is indicated by *u*; thus "Heracles" (hĕr′a-klēz) and "Hercules" (hur′kū-lēz). Otherwise, no attempt is made to indicate the various sounds of "short" vowels, but of course the *a* of "Pan" is not the same as the *a* of "Argus."

There are many books available for the reader who wishes more detailed accounts of the myths. H. J. Rose's *Handbook of Greek Mythology* (New York: E. P. Dutton & Co., Inc., 1950) and, for an authoritative and detailed account, W. H. Roscher's *Ausführliches Lexikon der Griechischen und Römischen Mythologie* (Leipzig: B. G. Teubner, 1884–1937) are recommended. A good introduction to the use of myths in English literature can be found in *Classical Myths in English Literature* (New York: Rinehart & Company, Inc., 1952), by Dan S. Norton and Peters Rushton, and for further study in this field two books by Douglas Bush are invaluable: *Mythology and the Renaissance Tradition in English Poetry* (New York: Pageant Book Co., 1933), and *Mythology and the Romantic Tradition in English Poetry* (New York: Pageant Book Co., 1937). The author wishes to express his warm gratitude to Professor Bush, who read this book in manuscript and made a large number of valuable criticisms and suggestions. Thanks are due also to Patricia Kirkwood and to Professor Harry Caplan, for salutary advice and for help in reading proof.

G.M.K.

May, 1959

NOTE ON THE 1995 EDITION

This new printing is essentially unchanged; some misprints and other errors have been noted on the appropriate pages.

Among recent general accounts of the subject Fritz Graf's *Greek Mythology* (English translation 1993) is especially recommended. As an extensive sourcebook, *Mythologies*, edited by Yves Bonnefoy and Wendy Doniger, is now available in addition to Roscher. The multi-volume, illustrated *Lexicon Iconographicum Mythologiae Graecae* is an exhaustive register of myth in ancient Greek art; it is now complete through Theseus. Ken Dowden's *The Uses of Greek Mythology* (Routledge, 1992) provides a good introduction to modern approaches. Mary Lefkowitz's *Women in Greek Myth* (London, 1986), Jan Bremmer's *Interpretations of Greek Mythology* (London, 1986), and Lowell Edmunds's *Approaches to Greek Myth* (Baltimore 1990) are useful studies of special aspects and approaches.

A SHORT GUIDE TO CLASSICAL MYTHOLOGY

Absyrtus (ab-sir′tus) was Medea's brother. See **Argonauts** (*Colchis*).

Acastus (a-kas′tus) was a king of Thessaly. For the story of him, his wife, and Peleus, see **Salmoneus.**

Acestes (a-ses′tēz), king of Drepanum, Sicily, entertained **Aeneas** (*Wanderings*).

Achates (a-kā′tēz) was the constant companion of Aeneas.

Achelous (ak-e-lō′us), a river god, wrestled with **Heracles** for the hand of Deianira, and lost.

Acheron (ak′e-ron) was one of the rivers in the realm of **Hades** (*Underworld*).

Achilles (a-kil′ēz), a Greek warrior, was the greatest hero of the **Trojan War.**

Acis (ā′sis) was the lover of the Nereid Galatea. See **Sea Deities.**

Acontius (a-kon′ti-us), of the island of Ceos, loved Cydippe, the daughter of rich parents who would not permit her to marry him. Acontius threw an apple to Cydippe, on which was written, "I swear by Artemis to marry no one but Acontius." Cydippe read the inscription to herself aloud (as was the usual practice in antiquity). When, subsequently, her parents sought to marry her to other men, Cydippe would grow ill each time the wedding approached. At last the parents consulted an oracle, learned that Cydippe's oath was binding, and permitted her to marry Acontius. The principal version of the story in ancient literature is Ovid's, in the *Heroides.* William Morris tells the story at length in *The Earthly Paradise* (1868–1870).

Acrisius (a-kris′i-us) was the father of Danae. See **Perseus.**

Actaeon (ak-tē′on) was turned into a stag by **Artemis** and killed by his own hounds.

Admetus (ad-mē′tus) was the husband of **Alcestis.**

Adonis (a-dō′nis), beloved of **Aphrodite,** was killed while hunting.

Adrastus (a-dras'tus) was the leader of the Seven against **Thebes.**

Aeacides (ē-as'i-dēz) means son of **Aeacus,** but is applied to Achilles and Ajax, grandsons of Aeacus.

Aeacus (ē'a-kus), son of Zeus and the nymph Aegina (eponym of the island of that name), married Endeis, daughter of the centaur Chiron (or of the robber Sciron, whom Theseus killed). Their children were Peleus and Telamon. By another wife, Psamathe, Aeacus had a son Phocus. Phocus was murdered by his two half-brothers, who consequently went into exile, Peleus into Thessaly (see the story of Acastus, Hippolyte, and Peleus, under **Salmoneus**), Telamon to the island of Salamis. Peleus and Telamon both took part in the expedition of the Argonauts and in the Calydonian Boar Hunt. For Peleus' marriage to Thetis and for their son Achilles, see **Trojan War** (*Background*). Telamon married Periboea, and by her had as son the great Ajax of the Trojan War. Telamon accompanied **Heracles** (ninth Labor) in his expedition against Troy, was given Hesione by him, and had a son Teucer, also a hero of the Trojan War, by Hesione. Aeacus was famous as a just man. On one occasion, when all Greece was suffering from famine, the country was saved by the intercession of his prayers to the gods. Another time, when the inhabitants of Aegina had died of a plague, Zeus replaced them by turning ants into human beings. These were the Myrmidons ("ant" in Greek is *myrmex*), who went to Thessaly with Peleus and were the soldiers of Achilles at Troy. Aeacus became, after his death, one of the three judges who assign to the dead their proper places in the underworld.

Aeetes (ē-ē'tēz) was the father of Medea. See **Argonauts** (*Colchis*).

Aegaeon (ē-jē'on), also known as Briareus, was one of the hundred-handed giants, sons of **Earth and Sky.**

Aegeus (ē'jūs) was the father of **Theseus.**

Aegina (ē-ji'na) is the name of an island near Athens, and of the eponymous nymph of it, mother of **Aeacus** by Zeus.

The **Aegis** (ē'jis) was a protective cloak or shield worn by **Zeus** (see beginning of article) and Athena.

Aegisthus (ē-jis'thus) was the son of Thyestes, and the lover of Clytemnestra. See **Atreus.**

Aeneas (ē-nē'as) was the founder of the Roman people and the hero of the most important of all Roman stories (some of the component parts of which are to be found also in Greek writers) and of the great epic poem of Virgil, the

Aeneid. He was the son of Aphrodite and the Trojan prince Anchises. For the story of his birth, see **Aphrodite.**

Aeneas was in the Trojan War but was not very conspicuous; twice he was saved in battle by the intervention of his goddess mother, once from Ajax and once from Achilles. The story of his escape from Troy with his father Anchises, his son Ascanius, and a group of followers is mentioned under **Trojan War** (*The fall*).

There follows a period of wandering and attendant adventure, in external appearance like the story of Odysseus' wanderings, just as the story of the troubles of Aeneas and his men in Italy, which are the subject of the second half of the *Aeneid,* is externally like the story of fighting at Troy told in the *Iliad*. But fundamentally the story of Aeneas, as told by Virgil, is unique: Aeneas is neither a shrewd, resourceful, inquisitive adventurer like Odysseus, nor a brilliant and violent warrior hero like Achilles; he is in search of *home*, he is the man of piety, gravity, and responsibility. The picture of him as he leaves Troy, with his aged father on his back, his son led by the hand, his household gods carefully preserved, typifies Aeneas.

Wanderings. Aeneas and his group land first in Thrace, meaning to settle there, but are driven away from the place when they find that it is accursed: Aeneas plucks a young shoot from the ground, and is horrified to find that it bleeds; then he hears a mournful voice from the ground, warning them to leave; it is the voice of Polydorus, youngest son of Priam, sent here for safety during the war but murdered by King Polymestor for the gold that he brought with him. Next they call at Delos, to consult Apollo about where they should go to find their new home. Misinterpreting the oracle, they believe that the god instructs them to go to Crete. When they try to settle in Crete, they are driven away by a pestilence. In a vision, Aeneas receives instructions to go west, to Italy. Next they visit the island of the Harpies, the hideous bird-women who figure also in the story of the Argonauts; they receive further prophecies from the Harpy Celaeno. They make a stop at Epirus, where they see Andromache and Helenus, now living there together, Neoptolemus having been killed. Their next stop is in Sicily, where, after a narrow escape from Charybdis, they pick up a Greek, Achaemenides, who was left there, in the land of the Cyclopes, by Odysseus and his men when they fled. After a stop in the west of Sicily at the kingdom of Drepanum, ruled by Acestes, where Anchises dies, they are blown off course and carried to the shore of Africa, in the vicinity of Carthage. The storm which drives them has been raised by Neptune at the request of Juno, who hates the Trojans and constantly hampers their efforts to establish a new home.

At Carthage they are kindly treated by the queen, Dido. At a great banquet, Aeneas tells the story of the fall of Troy and his subsequent adventures. By a trick of Venus, who wants to secure for her son and his men a cordial welcome, Dido falls hopelessly in love with Aeneas, and believes that he will stay there to become her consort. But Aeneas is finally forced to leave, by the will of the gods: Jupiter sends Mercury to order him to go. Dido commits suicide in grief and frenzy.

Italy. After another brief stay in Sicily, they make their way to Italy, first to Cumae, near Naples, where the Cumaean Sibyl guides Aeneas to the underworld. Aeneas here sees many denizens of the underworld, even as Odysseus does on his visit, and he sees, too, many spirits of illustrious Romans to be, and hears from Anchises, whom he has gone to the underworld to consult, prophecies of Rome's coming greatness.

The rest of Aeneas' adventures take place in the region of Latium, near the site of Rome. At first King Latinus and his subjects, the natives of the area, welcome the Trojans, and Lavinia, daughter of Latinus, is betrothed to Aeneas. But Juno, implacable in her hatred of the Trojans, again stirs up trouble. She rouses Queen Amata, wife of Latinus, to frenzy by sending to her the Fury Alecto. Amata had always favored as spouse for Lavinia the leader of the neighboring Rutulians, Turnus. War breaks out between the Trojans, with their allies the Etruscans, and the Latins and their allies, who include Turnus and his men, the beautiful maiden warrior Camilla, Mezentius, exiled Etruscan king, and his son Lausus. Various incidents of bravery and adventure take place. On a night raid two of Aeneas' men, devoted friends, Nisus and Euryalus, lose their lives after wreaking havoc among the enemy. Nisus, the elder of the two, could have got away, but turns back when Euryalus is trapped, and gives his life to gain revenge by killing the man who has killed his friend. The son of Aeneas and Creusa, Ascanius, who is also called Iulus (eponym of the Julian family, from whom the emperor Augustus had descent on the maternal side), performs various deeds of boyish prowess. Pallas, son of Aeneas' ally Evander, an Arcadian living at the place where Rome will later be, is killed by Turnus. The wicked King Mezentius, wounded by Aeneas, is aided by his son Lausus, and both father and son are killed. Finally there is a duel between Aeneas and Turnus in which Turnus is killed. Juno now capitulates, on terms: the Latins and the Trojans are to be joined under Aeneas, but the name of Trojans is to be given up. Aeneas marries Lavinia and founds the city of Lavinium.

The principal literary work embodying the story is, of course, Virgil's *Aeneid.* The *Inferno* of Dante's *Divine Comedy* owes much to Aeneas' descent to the underworld (*Aeneid,* 6). The story of Dido and Aeneas is a favorite subject; see, for example, Chaucer, *The Legend of Good Women,* and Purcell's opera, *Dido and Aeneas.*

Aeolus (ē'ō-lus) (1), son of Hellen (for whom see **Deucalion**), as well as being the eponym of the Aeolian branch of the Greek race, was the progenitor of a family of mythologically important persons. The Aeolids, as they are called, are a genealogical group about as important as the geographical groups under Athens and Thebes, though there is less continuity and connection among the stories. Of the twelve children of Aeolus, six are important enough to need mention. There were five sons: **Athamas; Salmoneus;** Cretheus, who was the father of Pheres (for whom see **Alcestis**) and Hippolyte (see **Salmoneus**); Perieres, who was the father of Tyndareus (for whom see **Leda**); and Sisyphus, famous for his cunning and for his punishment (for which see **Hades,** *Underworld*). There was one daughter, **Alcyone.**

Aeolus (2) was the king of the winds. See **Wind Deities.**

Aesculapius (es-kū-lā′pi-us) is the Roman form of Asclepius. See **Apollo** (end of the article).

Aeson (ē′son) was the father of Jason. See **Argonauts** (*Background*).

Agamemnon (ag-a-mem′non), son of **Atreus,** was king of Mycenae and leader of the Greeks in the **Trojan War.**

Aganippe (ag-a-nip′ē) was a spring on Mount Helicon, sacred to the Muses.

Agave (a-gā′vē) was the mother of Pentheus, victim of **Dionysus.**

Agenor (a-jē′nor), king of Tyre, was father of Europa of **Crete** and Cadmus of **Thebes.**

The **Ages of Man.** In Hesiod's poem *Works and Days,* the history of man is represented as consisting of five ages, each inferior to the one before. The first was the Golden Age, when Cronus was ruler of the universe. Men lived free of sorrow, labor, disease, and old age, and the earth produced abundant fruit unforced. When men died they became some kind of beneficent spirits and guardians of mankind. The men of the Silver Age were much inferior, living a hundred years of helpless infancy, followed by a brief maturity in which they were unjust to one another and impious to the gods; yet at their death they became spirits of the underworld, honored, though less honored than those of the Golden Age. Third came the Bronze Age, when men were mighty of strength, with weapons and implements of bronze; they died by one another's hands and disappeared altogether at death. Then came the Age of Heroes, who were demigods. They too were warriors, but nobler and more just than those of the Age of Bronze. They lived in the time of the heroic fighting at Thebes and Troy, and when they died they were granted an after-life of bliss in the Islands of the Blest, by the streams of Oceanus, where Cronus rules over them. Finally came the Age of Iron, in which men still languish. Life has become full of sorrow and toil, and man's moral nature has disintegrated; treachery and violence abound, even between parent and child, guest and host. Astraea, goddess of justice, left the earth when the Age of Iron began. In Hesiod's pessimistic account the harking back to a better day seems to reflect an awareness of the Mycenaean Age, as viewed from the troubled and unsettled Dark Age in which he lived.

In Ovid's *Metamorphoses*, 1, a different version of the Ages of Man appears. Here there are only four ages, Gold, Silver, Bronze, and Iron. The degeneration is more gradual, and though the Age of Iron is evil as in Hesiod, there is apparent in Ovid another pattern besides the increase of labor and sorrow and the loss of moral virtue; there is some emphasis also on the increasing complexity and skills of civilization, as men learn to live with the increasingly harsh circumstances of life.

Echoes of the ancient descriptions of the Golden Age are found in Chaucer's *The Former Age* and Milton's *Paradise Lost*. The idea of the coming of an age that recalls the Golden Age is found in Virgil's *Fourth Eclogue*, Milton's *On the Morning of Christ's Nativity*, and the final chorus of Shelley's *Hellas*.

Aglaia (a-glā′a) was one of the three **Charites** (Graces).

Aglaurus (a-glaw′rus) was a daughter of Cecrops, king of Athens. See **Ares, Athena,** and **Hermes.**

Aias (ā′as) is the Greek form of **Ajax.**

Ajax (ā′jax) (1), son of Telamon, was a great Greek warrior in the **Trojan War;** (2) Ajax, son of Oileus, from Locris, was also a Greek warrior at Troy.

Alcestis (al-ses′tis), daughter of King Pelias of Thessaly, was the wife of the Thessalian prince Admetus. Pelias offered his daughter in marriage to whoever could yoke a lion and a boar. Admetus succeeded, helped by Apollo, who was at that time serving a year of slavery to Admetus as punishment for having killed the Cyclopes (see **Apollo,** end of article). Admetus was a kind master, and in gratitude Apollo aided him in this task and granted him a further favor: if he could find somebody to substitute for him, he might live beyond the time appointed for him to die. The appointed time came soon, because Artemis was angry with Admetus for not having invited her to his wedding feast. Admetus searched for a substitute, but all refused—his father Pheres, his mother, all others except his beautiful young wife, who offered freely to die for him. The fatal day came, Alcestis died, and was carried in funeral procession to her grave. It chanced that that very day Heracles, in his travels, sought hospitality at the home of Admetus; not wanting to fail in his obligation as a host, Admetus concealed his grief and told Heracles only that he was in mourning for a woman of the household. Heracles proceeded to dine festively, even boisterously, until he learned from the grieving and offended servants the truth of the situation. At once Heracles set out to right matters: going to the tomb of Alcestis he found Thanatus (Death) waiting for her, wrestled with him for possession of Alcestis, was victorious, and restored Alcestis alive to Admetus.

On Euripides' *Alcestis* depend the numerous later versions. Among those in English are William Morris's *The Love of Alcestis* (in *The Earthly Paradise*, 1868–1870), Browning's *Balaustion's Adventure* (1871), John Todhunter's *Alcestis* (1879), and Carlota Montenegro's *Alcestis* (1909).

Alcides (al-sī'dēz) is another name for **Heracles.**

Alcinous (al-sin'ō-us), king of the Phaeacians, was host to **Odysseus** (*Sea adventures*).

Alcmaeon (alk-mē'on) was son of Amphiaraus of the Seven against **Thebes.**

Alcmena (alk-mē'na) was Heracles' mother by Zeus.

Alcyone (al-sī'ō-nē), daughter of Aeolus, and her husband the Thessalian king Ceyx were so proud of their royal position that they called each other Zeus and Hera. For this impiety, Zeus changed them into sea birds, the halcyon and the ceyx. Ovid (*Metamorphoses*, 11) tells a different and much more elaborate story about them: Ceyx was drowned at sea in a storm; his dying prayer was that Alcyone should find his body and give it proper burial. In a vision, Alcyone saw her husband's body floating in the sea, and rushed at once to the shore, where the vision became reality. Frantic with grief, Alcyone was plunging into the waves to her death, when she was transformed into a halcyon, and her husband into a ceyx. "Halcyon Days" are named for Alcyone; they are the fourteen days around the winter solstice, when the sea is traditionally calm, and when the halcyon is said to nest on the waves. Chaucer has the Ovidian version of the story in *The Book of the Duchess*.

Alecto (a-lek'tō), one of the Furies (see **Hades,** *Underworld*), appears in the story of **Aeneas** (*Italy*).

Alexander is another name for Paris of the **Trojan War.**

Alpheus (al-fē'us), an Arcadian river god, loved Arethusa. See **Sea Deities.**

Althea (al-thē'a) was the mother of Meleager of the **Calydonian Boar Hunt.**

Amalthea (am-al-thē'a) was the goat that nursed **Zeus.**

Amata (a-mā'ta) was the wife of King Latinus, in the story of **Aeneas** (*Italy*).

Amazons were a tribe of female warriors who lived to the east of the Greek regions of Asia Minor. The name means "breastless," and tradition had it that these women cut off their right breast in order to be able to use the bow more easily. In ancient art, however, the Amazons are regularly shown with normal breasts. The Amazons had no dealings with men except for breeding and as opponents in war. They reared only their female young. As warriors they keep recurring in Greek stories. Perseus, Heracles, and Bellerophon all fight against them, and Theseus abducts their queen, Hippolyte, or Antiope, in return for which the Amazons invade Attica. They are at the siege of Troy, as allies of the Trojans, under their queen, Penthesilea.

Ambrosia (am-brō'zi-a) was the food of the gods.

Ammon (am'on) was an Egyptian and Libyan god whom the Greeks identified with Zeus.

Amphiaraus (am-fē-a-rā'us) was one of the Seven against **Thebes.**

Amphion (am-fi'on), son of Zeus and Antiope, was a musician and builder of the walls of **Thebes.**

Amphitrite (am-fi-tri'tē) was the wife of **Poseidon.**

Amphitryon (am-fi'tri-on), a hero in his own right, was husband of Alcmena, mother of **Heracles** (*Background*).

Anchises (an-kī'sēz) was the father of **Aeneas.**

Androgeus (an-droj'e-us) was the son of Minos of Crete. See **Theseus** (*Minotaur*).

Andromache (an-drom'a-kē) was the wife of Hector during the **Trojan War.**

Andromeda (an-drom'e-da) was rescued by **Perseus** and became his wife.

Anna was the sister of Dido, whom Aeneas visited.

Antaeus (an-tē'us) was a giant son of Earth, defeated by **Heracles** (*Minor stories*).

Antenor (an-tē'nor) was a Trojan who escaped at the sack of Troy and founded a city in north Italy.

Anteros (an-těr'os) was the brother of **Eros.**

Antigone (an-tig'o-nē) was the daughter of Oedipus of **Thebes.**

Antilochus (an-til'o-kus), the son of Nestor, was killed by Memnon in the **Trojan War** (*Late events*).

Antinous (an-tin'ō-us) was one of Penelope's suitors in the story of **Odysseus** (*Ithaca*).

Antiope (an-tī'ō-pē) was (1) the mother of twins, Amphion and Zethus of **Thebes,** by Zeus; (2) a queen of the Amazons, abducted by **Theseus** (*Later adventures*).

Aphrodite (af-rō-di'tē), Roman Venus, is the goddess of love. She is called Cyprian because she was especially worshiped on the island of Cyprus, and Paphian from the city of Paphos on that island; the Romans sometimes called her Venus Erycina, from Mount Eryx in west Sicily, an old Carthaginian center of the worship of a goddess like Venus. The worship of Aphrodite on Cyprus probably had connections with Semitic and other Near Eastern religions; the Phoenician goddess Astarte is often identified or confused with Aphrodite. Aphrodite is called the Cytherean from the island of Cythera, where she first set foot after her birth in the sea.

Aphrodite is represented as a lovely woman, youthful but not girlish; in art she is usually nude, or nearly so, especially in later antiquity and thereafter. In Homer she is the possessor of a magic girdle of aphrodisiac power; in the *Iliad* Hera borrows it to deflect Zeus from thoughts of battle to thoughts of love. She probably derived some of her characteristics and powers from Near Eastern **Mother-Goddesses,** as the stories of her affairs with Adonis and Anchises, told below, indicate.

The story of her birth from the severed genitals of Uranus and the foam of the sea is told under **Cronus.** In Homer she is daughter of Zeus and the almost unknown goddess Dione. She is usually the wife of Hephaestus, but not a very faithful wife. Her most usual partner in intrigue is Ares. On one famous occasion, delightfully recorded in the *Odyssey*, Helius spied the guilty lovers in each other's arms and told Hephaestus. Hephaestus made a net of bronze and cast it about them while they slept. While they lay thus trapped and exposed, the gods came by and laughed and joked at their expense, though not all were without envy of Ares' plight. By Ares Aphrodite was the mother of Harmonia of Thebes; to Hermes she bore Hermaphroditus, whose story is told under **Hermes.**

Aphrodite's most celebrated love affair was a sad one. Adonis, son of **Cinyras** and Myrrha, was a handsome young hunter, with no interest in love. Aphrodite, after wounding herself in the breast with one of Eros's love-inflicting arrows, saw the youth and fell deeply in love with him. Adonis was unresponsive; he preferred to hunt. Aphrodite urged him to be cautious in the hunt, but Adonis was reckless, and at last was gored to death by a wild boar (sometimes said to have been sent by, or even to have *been*, the jealous Ares). Aphrodite wept long and bitterly for her lost darling, and caused a blood-red flower, the anemone, to grow from his blood. (This story has the earmarks of having sprung from a religious ritual connected with fertility: the death of a beautiful youth, and the prolonged lament for him. In some versions Adonis, born from a balsam tree, into which his mother was changed, was reared by Aphrodite, or was given by her to Persephone to rear; Persephone loved him and would not give him back. Finally a compromise was arranged whereby Adonis should spend two thirds of the year with Aphrodite, one third with Persephone.)

In punishment for Aphrodite's cruelty in inflicting love upon the other gods, Zeus caused her to fall in love with a mortal, the Trojan prince Anchises. Disguised as a mortal huntress, she seduced Anchises, revealing her divinity before she left. She warned him never to reveal that he had lain with Aphrodite. When Anchises later did tell, his punishment was to be stricken with paralysis from the waist down. Aeneas was the son of their union.

One of the most famous favorites of Aphrodite was Paris, the Trojan prince. Here she appears not as his mistress but as the sponsor of love, helping him to abduct and keep Helen (see **Trojan War**). In the poetry of Homer Aphrodite is not an impressive figure; she is even wounded in battle by the Greek hero Diomedes.

Eros, the god of love, Roman Cupid, is the constant attendant of Aphrodite.

In Roman literature Venus is sometimes a dignified mother figure, as she is in the *Aeneid*. As mother of Aeneas she is in some sense the mother of the Romans.

Important ancient poems concerning Aphrodite, in addition to the *Aeneid*, are the *Homeric Hymn to Aphrodite* (Aphrodite and Anchises), the *Odyssey*, 8 (Aphrodite, Ares, and Hephaestus), and Ovid's *Metamorphoses*, 10 (Venus and Adonis). Shakespeare's *Venus and Adonis* is one of numerous treatments of the theme in English poetry; see also Spenser, *The Faerie Queene*, 3. 1, 6.

Apollo (a-pol'ō), son of Zeus and Leto, twin brother of Artemis, typifies one side, and that the more characteristic, of classical Greek civilization. He is the perpetually vigorous and graceful young man. In contrast to his half-brother Dionysus, the wild and enthusiastic zealot, Apollo is calm and orderly, but the calm is not the quiet of lethargy; there is a powerful tension, a balance of vigor and reason. In art Apollo has flowing hair, usually bound by a laurel wreath; he carries a bow or lyre, and may be robed or nude. He is the god of music and poetry, of archery, and of prophecy, especially at his great shrine at Delphi. Sudden death through disease is the attack of the arrows of Apollo; but Apollo is also a god of healing, though his son Asclepius (see below) largely takes over this function. Apollo was from early times a god of purity and radiance, but he was not specifically connected with the sun before the fifth century B.C.

He is called Phoebus chiefly in his role of god of light, and chiefly, in antiquity, by the Romans, who apart from this had no separate name for him. He is called Delian from Delos, the island where he was born; he is Cynthian from Mount Cynthus on Delos. He is Delphian and Pythian from his shrine at Delphi. He is called Paean in his capacity of a healing god; and the kind of poem called a paean was originally associated with his worship.

Leto, Roman Latona, daughter of the Titans Coeus and Phoebe, when pregnant by Zeus wandered everywhere seeking a place where her offspring might be born. Because of Hera's jealousy, all places were afraid to receive her, until at last the little island of Delos gave her refuge, and here her twin children, Artemis and Apollo, were born. Delos long remained a great center of the worship of Apollo. The other place most particularly associated with him is Delphi, on the side of Mount Parnassus in central Greece. Here Apollo killed a serpent called the Python, and established a great prophetic shrine. Sometimes it is said that the Titaness Themis had the shrine before him, and this, as well as the killing of the Python, suggests that Apollo took over a place already of religious significance, associated with chthonic (i.e., earth) powers. The priestess of Apollo at Delphi, who chanted in verse the oracles of the god, was called the Pythia. Here was located the Omphalus, a stone which marked the center of the world. There were other, less-known oracular shrines of Apollo—Clarus, Branchidae, and Patara, all in southern Asia Minor, and one near Troy, from which he is called Thymbraean Apollo. Apollo had also a connection with the people known as the Hyperboreans, whose name suggests that they lived beyond the north wind; they spent their days in feasting, and Apollo loved them dearly.

The loves of Apollo were numerous. Most famous of all is the story of Daphne, daughter of the river god Peneus. Ovid says that Apollo, when he beheld her, had been struck by one of Cupid's golden, love-enkindling arrows, while Daphne had been struck by a leaden one, and fled the ardent god. She was, too, a devotee of Artemis, and so vowed to chastity. As the fleet god was about to overcome the maiden in their chase, she prayed to her father that her beauty might be so changed as to spare her from the god's embrace. At once she was transformed into a laurel tree (*daphne* is Greek for laurel) and the god henceforth made the laurel his sacred tree and wreathed his hair with its branches.

For a god of such beauty, Apollo was singularly unsuccessful in love affairs. He sought the favors of the maiden Marpessa, and had as a rival for her hand the mortal Idas, one of the Argonauts. Idas stood his ground against the god, and when they were about to engage in combat for her, Zeus parted them and bade Marpessa choose between them. She chose the mortal, fearing that the ever-youthful Apollo would desert her when she grew old. Another love of Apollo was the Trojan princess Cassandra (see also **Trojan War**). He bestowed upon her the gift of prophecy, but when she refused his love he added a penalty: no one should believe her prophecies. A somewhat similar affair involves the Sibyl of Cumae. (The name Sibyl probably means prophetess, and was applied to many persons, of whom the Sibyl of Cumae, guide of Aeneas in his journey to the underworld, is the best known; the Sibylline Books, which were actually in existence and were consulted by the Romans as late as the time of Augustus, were ascribed to her.) Apollo loved her and granted her extreme longevity, but withheld, when she withheld her favors, prolonged youth. And so the Sibyl lived a thousand years, and became a tiny shriveled creature in a bottle who had only one wish, to die. (Cf. Tithonus, under **Sky Deities.**) More successful was Apollo's suit of Cyrene, a nymph whom he beheld wrestling a lion and fell in love with. He carried her off from Mount Pelion to Libya, where the city of Cyrene was named for her. Born of their union was the minor agricultural deity Aristaeus. On one occasion Apollo was enamored of a handsome boy, Hyacinthus; the boy was killed when struck by a discus thrown by Apollo himself; it was an accident, of course, unless Zephyrus, the west wind, out of jealousy deliberately forced the discus toward the youth. From the blood of the dying youth sprang a flower, marked with a sign resembling a Greek exclamation of sorrow, and still called by his name. (The beautiful youth who dies suggests that the story originated in a ritual concerning agricultural growth.)

There are stories, too, about Apollo's musical prowess. The satyr Marsyas, who prided himself on his skill as a flutist, challenged Apollo to a contest of musical skill, the winner to do as he chose with the loser. Marsyas of course lost, and was flayed alive. Pan also challenged Apollo. On this occasion Mount Tmolus, in Lydia, was the judge, and he declared Apollo the winner; King Midas of Phrygia, who was present, criticized the judge's decision, and Apollo, in a fury, changed Midas's ears to ass's ears. Midas thenceforth kept his ears covered by a turban, swearing his barber, who alone knew the truth, to secrecy. The barber longed to tell someone, and finally dug a hole in the ground and whispered the secret into it. He filled in the hole, but reeds grew on the spot, and whenever the wind passed through them they whispered sibilantly, "King Midas has ass's ears."

This is the Midas of the golden touch. As a reward for a favor, Dionysus once granted Midas the fulfillment of any one wish. The acquisitive Midas rashly wished that everything that he touched might turn to gold. After a brief period of delight he soon regretted his wish, when his food, his drink, and finally his affectionate daughter became gold at his touch. And so he begged to be rid of his gift, and was granted the privilege of washing it off in the Pactolus River, which ever after had sands of gold, from Midas's transferred power.

Asclepius, Roman Aesculapius, god of medicine, was Apollo's son, by another unhappy love affair. Coronis, a Thessalian girl, was dearly beloved of Apollo, until the raven, who had at that time white plumage, spied her in the arms of another youth and told Apollo. In swift fury Apollo shot an arrow into the breast of Coronis, and as she lay dying at once regretted his hasty vengeance. He was unable, for all his medical skill, to save her, but he did save her unborn child and his, Asclepius. The raven's plumage he turned black, for its part in the matter. As a child, Asclepius was trained by the wise centaur Chiron, who taught him a knowledge of herbs and surgery. When he became a man, so great was his skill that at the request of Artemis he even undertook to restore Hippolytus to life (see **Theseus**). Zeus would not have this, and blasted Asclepius to Tartarus with a thunderbolt. In reprisal, Apollo killed the Cyclopes who had made the thunderbolt, for which deed he had to serve a year of bondage to a mortal (see **Alcestis**).

Apollo is sometimes said to be the father of Linus and Mopsus, famous in mythology as musician and prophet, respectively. No more than mention is needed here of two other stories: when Tityus (see **Hades,** *Underworld*) attempted to rape Leto, it was Apollo who killed him with an arrow. He and Artemis on one other famous occasion shot their arrows on behalf of their mother; see the story of Niobe, under **Thebes.** The story of Clytia and that of Phaethon are sometimes connected with Apollo, but they really concern Helius, the sun god; see under **Sky Deities.**

See, in ancient literature, the *Homeric Hymn to Apollo* and the story of Daphne in Ovid's *Metamorphoses*, 1; in English literature, Keats, *Hyperion* (Apollo as the ideal poet of tragic knowledge), Shelley, *Hymn of Apollo* (1820, mostly on Apollo as sun god), and poems called *Daphne* by George Meredith (1851) and Francis Thompson (1893).

Apsyrtus. See **Absyrtus.**

Aquilo (ak'wi-lō) is Boreas, the north wind. See **Wind Deities.**

Arachne (a-rak'nē) was turned into a spider by **Athena.**

Arcadia (ar-kā'di-a), the mountainous and thinly populated central province of the Peloponnesus, though much celebrated by poets of late antiquity and subsequent periods as the home of shepherds and shepherdesses living a life of song, comradeship, and leisure, has very few myths or mythological persons closely associated with it. The stories of Callisto and Coronis are told under **Artemis** and **Apollo,** respectively. The wicked King Lycaon, for whom see **Deucalion,** was an Arcadian. **Hermes** was born in a cave on Mount Cyllene, in Arcadia. The god most frequently and peculiarly associated with Arcadia is the strange woodland creature **Pan.**

Arcas (ar'kas) was the son of Callisto. See **Artemis.**

Ares (ar'ēz), Roman Mars, son of Zeus and Hera, is the god of war. He is not a major Greek deity, and even in the sphere of war is overshadowed by Athena and others. But as Roman Mars he is more substantial, partly, perhaps, as harmonizing better with the martial spirit of the Romans, but also because Mars was, in origin, a deity of wider scope than warfare, having also some functions as a god of agriculture. Mars is father of **Romulus,** founder of Rome. Companions of Ares and minor war deities are Enyo (female) and Enyalios (male).

Ares is not a very prominent character in myth. In the attack of Otus and Ephialtes against the gods (see under **Zeus**), he is sometimes said to have been held prisoner by the two giants until Hermes rescued him by stealth. He is the partner of Aphrodite in a love affair. For their entrapment by Hephaestus see under **Aphrodite.** By Aphrodite, Ares is sometimes said to be the father of Eros, the god of love, and Anteros.

Ares had a love affair with Aglaurus, one of the daughters of Cecrops, King of Athens. (For other stories concerning her and her sisters, see **Athena** and **Hermes.**) They had a daughter Alcippe. She was violated by a son of Poseidon named Halirrhothius, and in revenge Ares killed Halirrhothius. For this act he was tried in the Athenian court of the Areopagus ("Hill of Ares") before the assembled gods and acquitted.

Ares is father of various persons whose stories are told elsewhere, such as Harmonia (see **Thebes,** *Cadmus*), and Cycnus, a giant killed by **Heracles.**

Arethusa (ar-e-thū′za), a Nereid, was loved by Alpheus. See **Sea Deities.**

Argives (ar′jīvz), properly the men of Argos, are in Homer the Greeks in general.

The **Argo** (ar′gō) was the ship of the **Argonauts.**

The **Argonauts** (ar′gō-nots) were the mariners who, led by Jason, sailed east in the ship Argo in search of the Golden Fleece. One of the most popular of myths, the tale of their adventures has features of the "quest" theme, which it shares with the story of Perseus, and is also a story of travel related to the wanderings of Odysseus.

Background. The story begins with Phrixus and Helle, son and daughter of King Athamas of Orchomenus in Boeotia, who were rescued from their cruel stepmother Ino by a golden-fleeced flying ram, who carried them on his back to safety until Helle fell off and was drowned in a body of water thereafter called the Hellespont (now the Dardanelles). Phrixus landed in far-off Colchis, at the east end of the Black Sea. The ram was sacrificed to Zeus (strange reward for his services) and the fleece hung up in a sacred grove.

At about this time, Pelias, son of Poseidon, replaced, by succession or usurpation, his half-brother Aeson as king of a region in Thessaly. Jason, young son of Aeson, was removed by his mother from the dangerous vicinity of Pelias, and was sent to be trained in all manner of skills and arts by the centaur Chiron. Meanwhile Pelias sat on his throne uncomfortably, because it was predicted that a man with one sandal would depose him. In due course a stranger with one sandal appeared, and it was Jason, now grown to young manhood. He had lost a sandal in helping an old woman across a mountain torrent; the old woman was Hera in disguise, and she became henceforth Jason's ally. Pelias thought it well to be rid of this youth, and charged him to recover the Golden Fleece, saying that Phrixus' ghost asked that it be done.

And so the great expedition was organized. The ship was built by and named for Argus, son of Phrixus. Argus was helped by Athena, who in this story shares with Hera the role of sponsor of heroes. The crew consisted of the fifty foremost heroes of Greece, a list which varies in every ancient telling, but always includes such stalwarts as Castor and Polydeuces; Zetes and Calais (sons of Boreas, the north wind); Lynceus, the sharp-eyed lookout; Tiphys, the pilot; Heracles; Meleager and other figures of the Calydonian Boar Hunt; Amphiaraus of the Seven against Thebes; Admetus, husband of Alcestis; some fathers of leaders in the Trojan War such as Peleus, father of Achilles, and Telamon, father of Ajax; and, finally, the seer Mopsus and the musician Orpheus. The journey itself has three parts, the voyage to Colchis, the adventures there, and the return. Both the outward voyage and the return have been much elaborated by successive tellers of the story, but only a few incidents are important in mythology.

Outward voyage. Outward bound, the Argonauts set sail from Iolchus in Thessaly, and put in first at the island of Lemnos, where they found only women. The women of Lemnos had killed all their men for marital infidelity; only Queen Hypsipyle had saved and hidden her father Thoas, for which act of mercy she was later exiled (she reappears in the story of the Seven against **Thebes**). The Argonauts stayed on Lemnos a year, and sired a new generation of Lemnians. Jason had two sons by Hypsipyle. Next they * visited the land of the Doliones and King Cyzicus, where fighting broke out and the king was killed. Here, or at a stop soon after, Hylas, a very handsome young Argonaut, went to fetch water and was lost, drawn down into the pool by the water nymphs, who found his beauty irresistible. Heracles, who loved Hylas, would not leave without him, and while he searched in vain for him, the Argo went on. For the story of the Argonauts, or for Jason's pre-eminence in it, this was good riddance, since Heracles in a subordinate role in adventure could be only an embarrassment. Next they came to the land of the Bebrycians, whose king, Amycus, was a mighty pugilist and challenged any of the Argonauts to a boxing match. Polydeuces, the great boxer, accepted the challenge and killed Amycus with one blow. In Salmydessus (the geography is vague, but all these places are in the eastern Aegean and the approaches to the Black Sea) they encountered the blind King Phineus, who was persecuted by hideous bird-women, the Harpies, who snatched his food from his table, or fouled it with their droppings. His sufferings are variously accounted for; one story is that he had, at the urging of his wife Idaea, blinded the two sons of his first wife Cleopatra. Phineus was a prophet, and in gratitude for help (Zetes and Calais chased away the Harpies) revealed how the Argonauts could pass their next obstacle, the Symplegades, or "Clashing Rocks," two great cliffs which ran together and crushed all ships that tried to pass. Following Phineus' advice, the Argonauts got through, though Athena (or Hera) had to sit at the stern and hold the rocks apart for a crucial moment.

Colchis. Arrived at Colchis, Jason demanded the Fleece of Aeetes, who promised to yield it if Jason could yoke two fire-breathing, brazen-footed bulls, plow a field with them, and sow the field with dragon's teeth. Jason passed this test, with the aid of Aeetes' beautiful sorceress daughter, Medea,

*read: winged sons

who fell in love with the hero. She gave him a magic ointment to protect him against the fiery breath of the bulls, and told him how to subdue the crop of armed men who would at once spring up when the dragon's teeth were sown. Jason threw a stone into their midst, and thus set them fighting among themselves so violently that he could easily dispatch the weary survivors. Aeetes still demurred, and so Jason stole the Fleece by night, again aided by Medea, who lulled to sleep with a potion the serpent that guarded the Fleece. Off went the heroes in the Argo, and Medea went with them. Aeetes soon followed in hot pursuit, but was once more foiled by Medea, this time by the most bloodthirsty of all her exploits. She had prudently taken with her her young brother Absyrtus, and when Aeetes was about to overtake them, she chopped the boy into small pieces and flung them into the sea. While Aeetes paused to retrieve the fragments, the Argo got clear away.

Return voyage. The route of the return voyage is hopelessly confused. In one version or another the Argonauts navigated nearly all the known waters of the earth: the streams of Oceanus, the Danube, the Po, the Red Sea, etc. The incidents of the return are mostly duplications of the adventures of Odysseus or of the outward voyage: there is another set of clashing rocks, they encounter the Sirens (and are saved when Orpheus bests the Sirens' song by playing on his lyre), Scylla and Charybdis, and Circe, by whom they are purified from their murder of Absyrtus. At Crete they encountered the brazen giant Talos, who circled the coastline of the island as a sentry and dispatched all intruders. On Medea's advice, the Argonauts drained out of his body the divine fluid, ichor, which gave him life, by removing a secret plug in his heel after he had been drugged.

Thus the Fleece was returned to Thessaly, and the expedition of the Argonauts came to an end, but not the adventures of Jason and Medea. They found that the wicked Pelias had put to death Jason's parents, and Medea therefore wrought a terrible revenge, persuading Pelias' daughters to try to restore their father to youth. First she boiled an aged ram in a cauldron filled with magic herbs; presently out sprang the ram, young and vigorous. Then the daughters of Pelias tried the same experiment with their aged father, with Medea assisting. But Medea this time did not put the right herbs in the cauldron, and Pelias died. Jason and Medea found it prudent to leave Thessaly; Pelias was succeeded by his son Acastus.

Corinth. The last scene of Jason's career is the saddest, and the least creditable to him. After living at Corinth for some years with Medea and the two sons she had borne him, Jason decided to take a new wife, Glauce (or Creusa), daughter of King Creon of Corinth, either because he had tired of Medea and fallen in love with the princess, or because he wanted to better his position. Medea, infuriated but hiding her fury, sent a splendid tiara and robes as wedding gifts for the princess. When Glauce donned these garments they clung to her flesh and ate it away; she died in agony, as did her father too when he tried to free her from torment. Then Medea butchered her sons, as a punishment to Jason and to prevent their falling into the hands of the Corinthians. (In some versions the children were killed by the Corinthians.) Medea escaped in a chariot drawn by winged dragons and went to Athens, where Aegeus had previously committed himself to giving her sanctuary. After playing a slight part in the adventures of **Theseus** (*Early adventures*) Medea fled again, this time to Asia, where she became ancestress of the Medes. Jason eventually met undistinguished but fitting death. As Medea had prophesied, he was killed by a piece of wood which fell from the Argo, now rotting where he had set it as a dedication to Poseidon at the Isthmus of Corinth.

The story of the Argonauts has been told many times, in antiquity by the Greek epic poet Apollonius of Rhodes and the Roman Valerius Flaccus, both of whom wrote poems called *Argonautica*, and more allusively by Pindar in the *Fourth Pythian*. Chaucer has Hypsipyle and Medea in *The Legend of Good Women*. Longest of all poems on the subject is William Morris's *The Life and Death of Jason* (1867), in seventeen books. Robert Graves has the story in the likeness of a historical novel, *Hercules My Shipmate* (1945). The story of Jason and Medea has been a favorite dramatic subject ever since Euripides' *Medea;* subsequent versions include those of Seneca, Pierre Corneille (seventeenth century), Richard Glover (eighteenth century), Franz Grillparzer (early nineteenth century), and Jean Anouilh (twentieth century). Robinson Jeffers has written an adaptation of Euripides' play, and a modernized version of the story (*Solstice*, 1935).

Argus (ar′gus) was (1) the guardian of **Io;** (2) the dog of **Odysseus** (*Ithaca*); (3) the builder of the Argo, and an Argonaut.

Ariadne (ar-i-ad′nē) of Crete was the bride of both **Theseus** (*Minotaur*) and **Dionysus.**

The **Arimaspians** (ar-i-mas′pi-anz) were a fabulous one-eyed tribe who lived somewhere off to the north and east of the Greek settlements in Asia.

Arion (a-ri′on), son of **Poseidon** and Demeter, was the steed of Adrastus, of the Seven against **Thebes.**

Aristaeus (ar-is-tē′us) was a son of **Apollo,** and the pursuer of Eurydice (see **Orpheus**).

Artemis (ar′te-mis), Roman Diana, daughter of Zeus and Leto, twin sister of Apollo, is the virgin goddess of the hunt, and the protectress of wild animals, especially the young. Her protectiveness extends to the human young, and hence she is a goddess of birth and a goddess of women. She is an archer, and her shafts are sometimes said to bring sudden death from sickness to women, as those of Apollo do to men. She is often identified with the moon goddess (Selene, Luna), and sometimes with the nocturnal goddess Hecate, who is also sometimes a moon goddess. She is sometimes called Phoebe (as Apollo is Phoebus), though the name Phoebe is originally that of their Titan grandmother, mother of Leto. She is called Cynthia from Mount Cynthus on Delos, where she was born. Her place of birth is sometimes called Ortygia, but this usually means the same island as Delos. In any event, she was born before her twin brother, and helped her mother at his birth. (See further under **Apollo** for the story of their birth.) Artemis and Apollo are often together, in worship and in mythological incidents. Artemis is regularly represented as dressed for the hunt, with high boots and short tunic, carrying bow and quiver and accompanied by dogs. She is youthful, graceful, virginal.

Very different is the Ephesian Artemis, who was worshiped as a **Mother-Goddess,** and represented as a many-breasted symbol of fertility. It is possible that this figure is not just the result of Near Eastern influence, but preserves a side of Artemis that was originally present as a part of her role as protector and fosterer of the young, but became lost in Greek and Roman stories.

There are a number of stories of Artemis that represent her as a punisher or avenger. For instance, Orion, the giant son of Earth or of Poseidon, was killed by her archery when he offered violence to a Hyperborean maiden. (For the Hyperboreans see under **Apollo;** note that the twin deities share this interest.) Orion was a violent and ill-starred creature. For his adventures with Eos the dawn goddess and with the Pleiades, see under **Sky Deities.** He loved Merope, but her father Oenopion hated him, and blinded him after getting him drunk. Orion was healed, eventually, by the rays of Helius, the sun, only to suffer his mishaps with Eos and Artemis. Artemis' punishment of the Theban prince Actaeon is a good instance of the inhumanity of deity. While hunting, the young man, weary and in search of shade and water, chanced upon Artemis and her nymphs as they bathed, and his eyes beheld the goddess naked. For this involuntary offense the goddess caused him to be transformed into a stag and torn to pieces by his own hounds.

Artemis has nearly always a band of followers, usually described as nymphs. They are sworn to chastity but are not always able to keep their vows. One of the nymphs, Britomartis, was loved and pursued by King Minos of Crete. She leaped into the sea to escape him, and fell into a fisherman's net, from which she was renamed Dictynna (the Greek for net being *dictyon*), a name sometimes borne by Artemis herself. Another nymph, Callisto, was beloved of Zeus, who, by disguising himself as Artemis, was able to join the maiden group and seduce Callisto. When Callisto became obviously pregnant, she was driven from the group. The child was Arcas, ancestor of the Arcadians (Artemis and her nymphs are often associated with the groves and mountains of Arcadia). At some point Callisto was transformed into a bear by the jealous Hera, and for years wandered in the woods. Arcas grew up, and while hunting one day encountered a bear which fixed him with her gaze; for the animal was poor Callisto. Alarmed, Arcas was about to shoot the bear, when Zeus stayed his arm and lifted mother and son to the heavens, where she became Ursa Major and he Arcturus.

For the part of Artemis in the story of Niobe, see **Thebes.** The story of Endymion, which is sometimes associated with her, really belongs to Selene; see under **Sky Deities.**

Ascanius (as-cā'ni-us) was the son of **Aeneas** and Creusa.

Asclepius (as-clē'pi-us) was the god of medicine, son of **Apollo** (end of article).

Astarte (as-tar'tē) was a Phoenician goddess whom the Greeks identified with **Aphrodite.**

Astraea (as-trē'a), the goddess of justice, left the world of men at the beginning of the Age of Iron. See the **Ages of Man.**

Astyanax (as-tī'a-nax) was the son of the Trojan hero Hector.

Atalanta (at-a-lan'ta), daughter of Iasus, was exposed at birth; her father had wanted a boy. She was suckled by a she-bear, and grew up in the forests, becoming skilled in hunting and athletics. As a young woman, she rejoined her parents. Now her father wished her to marry, but Atalanta declined to marry any man who would not risk his life in a foot race with her: if he won he should have her as wife; if he lost he must die. Many tried and lost. Finally Hippomenes defeated her, with the help of Aphrodite, who gave him three golden apples. By throwing these off to the side of the racecourse at judicious intervals Hippomenes caused Atalanta to lose so much time retrieving the apples that he was able to win. They were married, and had as son Parthenopaeus, one of the Seven against Thebes. The conqueror and husband of Atalanta is sometimes called Milanion. According to Ovid, husband and wife were later both turned into lions drawing the chariot of Cybele; this was a punishment caused by Aphrodite because Hippomenes had not been properly grateful to her. Whether this Atalanta and the Atalanta of the **Calydonian Boar Hunt** are the same person is uncertain.

Atalanta's race is described in Ovid's *Metamorphoses*, 10; William Morris has a version in *The Earthly Paradise* (1868).

Ate (ā'tē) means delusion or infatuation. Though often personified as a minor deity, it is really a concept rather than a mythological figure.

Athamas (ath'a-mas), son of Aeolus, and king of Orchomenus in Boeotia, had, by his first wife, Nephele, two children, Phrixus and Helle. Athamas later married Ino of Thebes, who was the sister of Semele and thus the aunt of

Dionysus, whose nurse she had been for a while. Ino devised a step-motherly plot against Phrixus and Helle. She got the women of Orchomenus foolishly to parch the year's supply of seed grain before sowing it. Consequently there was no harvest that year. Ambassadors sent to Delphi to ask the oracle how to combat the resulting famine were bribed by Ino to bring back the false reply that Phrixus must be offered as a sacrifice. At the last moment a golden-fleeced ram saved Phrixus by carrying him, with Helle, away on its back. The rest of their story is told under **Argonauts** (*Background*). Athamas and Ino had two children, Learchus and Melicertes. Hera, hostile to Ino for her part in rearing Dionysus, drove both parents mad. Athamas, imagining that he was hunting, killed Learchus, and was pursuing Melicertes, when Ino leaped off a cliff into the sea with Melicertes in her arms. They became the minor **Sea Deities** Leucothea and Palaemon.

Athena (a-thē′na), Roman Minerva, is the protectress of cities and their rulers, goddess of craftsmanship (especially as Minerva, and especially of the arts of women), and goddess of wisdom. She is a virgin, and in art she appears as a youthful but dignified and stately figure, grey-eyed (*glaucopis*, which, however, perhaps means, rather, "gleaming-eyed"), usually in full armor, with tall helmet, long spear, shield, and aegis (for which see under **Zeus**). On shield or aegis the head of Medusa (see **Perseus**) usually appears. With her may be her special bird, the owl, and a snake may be coiled at her feet or beside her resting shield. In early Greek myth, in Homer for instance, she is chiefly a warrior and a protectress of heroes; in vase paintings she is often seen standing behind Perseus, Heracles, Bellerophon, or another hero. Later, and in Rome, the emphasis is on her wisdom and her skill in weaving and other crafts. Throughout ancient myth, she is closer to her father Zeus than is any of the other gods; she alone has the privilege of wearing her father's aegis. She is often called Pallas Athena; the significance of the name Pallas is unknown. Her title Tritogeneia ("Triton-born") perhaps suggests a connection with Triton, son of Poseidon, and with the sea. See also **Palladium.**

The most famous story about her is that of her birth. After Zeus had swallowed his first wife, Metis, Athena sprang, fully armed and shouting a battle cry, from his brow. (Sometimes it is said that Zeus suffered a headache and had Hephaestus or Prometheus cleave his brow with an axe.)

Athena is, of course, the patron deity of Athens. For the story of how she became so see under **Poseidon.** She is almost the ancestress of the Athenians: Hephaestus attempted to rape her, she resisted, and the god's semen fell upon the ground and fertilized it. From the ground was born the autochthonous (which means "sprung from the ground") Erichthonius, and Athena took him in charge. She put the baby in a basket and entrusted it to Pandrosus, daughter of Cecrops, the king of Athens; the sisters of Pandrosus, Aglaurus and Herse, peeped into the basket, against the express command of Athena, and in her anger the goddess caused the two girls to fling themselves from the Acropolis to death on the rocks below. Some versions have it that they were driven mad by what they saw in the basket; for Erichthonius had snake legs. But so had their father Cecrops. (Earthborn creatures often do, the Giants for example.).

The story of Arachne has to do with the weaving skill of Athena. Arachne was the most skillful of mortal weavers and boasted much of her art. Disguised as a crone, Athena came and warned her not to boast so much. When Arachne proved unteachable, Athena assumed her proper form and challenged the girl to a weaving contest. Athena wove designs portraying her victory over **Poseidon** in their contest for Athens, and others showing how mortals had been punished by the gods for presumptuousness; Arachne responded with pictures of various illicit love affairs of Zeus, Poseidon, and other gods. Furious, Athena tore Arachne's web and struck her with her spindle. In humiliation, Arachne hanged herself, but Athena saved her from death and turned her into a spider, ancestress of the arachnids.

Athens was not, in earliest times, as important a place as Thebes, Mycenae, and other cities, but because it later became the greatest of all centers of literary activity, its stories are among those most often told and widely known. The names of kings of even remoter antiquity are recorded, but Athenian mythological history really begins with King Cecrops, the snake-legged ruler. Snake-leggedness is a common sign of being autochthonous, sprung from the very ground on which one lives. The successor to Cecrops, Erichthonius, was also snake-legged and autochthonous. The story of his birth is told under **Athena**. Cecrops had three daughters, Aglaurus, Herse, and Pandrosus, all of some importance in myth. Stories concerning them are told under **Athena, Hermes,** and **Ares.** Son of Erichthonius and his wife, Pasithea, was Pandion, who had, by Zeuxippe, a son, Erechtheus, and two daughters, Procne and Philomela.

The story of Procne and Philomela is extremely familiar but often confused. Procne married King Tereus of Thrace. After a while, Procne's sister Philomela came to the wild north to visit them. (Or, Tereus tired of Procne, locked her away in a shack, and went and got Philomela, pretending that Procne wanted her to come for a visit.) Tereus was moved to passionate desire for Philomela, and, barbarian that he was, raped her and then cut out her tongue so that she could never tell. But Philomela managed to convey the tale to Procne by weaving it on a web, and the two sisters got together and plotted a terrible revenge on Tereus. They killed Itys or Itylus, Procne's own son by Tereus, and served him up to Tereus as food. Then they revealed to Tereus what he had eaten. Snatching a knife, Tereus started in pursuit of Procne and Philomela, and even as the chase went on, all three were transformed into birds, Tereus into a hawk or a hoopoe, Procne into a nightingale, mourning for her murdered child, Philomela into the chattering, speechless swallow. This is the standard story in nearly all ancient authors, though Ovid does not specify what birds the sisters became. Some Roman versions, and, following these, most later versions, make Philomela the wife and the nightingale, Procne the tongueless victim and the swallow. Sometimes, illogically, Philomela remains the victim and yet becomes the nightingale, Procne the wife and the swallow.

Erechtheus, son of Pandion, succeeded his father. In his time a war was fought between Athens and Eleusis, the home of the celebrated mysteries. Told by an oracle that the death of his daughter would ensure victory, Erechtheus sacrificed one of his daughters. The Eleusinians, led by Eumolpus, son of Poseidon, were defeated and Eumolpus was killed, but Poseidon avenged his son's death by killing Erechtheus.

Erechtheus had three other daughters who figure in myth, Creusa, Procris, and Orithyia. Creusa in her youth was seduced by Apollo and bore him a child, Ion. She exposed Ion, but he was taken by Hermes to Delphi, where he became a servant to the priestess in his father's temple. Creusa later married Xuthus, and they were childless. Going to Delphi to inquire how they might mend this state, Xuthus was told to hail as his son the first youth whom he met on leaving the temple. It was Ion whom he met and hailed. Creusa, unaware of Ion's identity, suspected that he was the child of an earlier liaison of Xuthus, and was about to poison the youth when he discovered her plot and was about to kill her. At this point, through Apollo's priestess, a recognition comes about between mother and son; Ion is accepted by her and Xuthus and later becomes king of Athens and founder of the Ionian branch of the Greek people.

Procris was married to Cephalus, for whose earlier affair with Eos see under **Sky Deities.** After various adventures, including an affair with King Minos of Crete, Procris settled down with Cephalus, but disaster followed. Cephalus, who was an ardent huntsman, possessed a spear that could not miss its mark. So much was he in the field that Procris suspected a rival and one day spied on her husband. Cephalus, tired out from hunting, lay down near Procris's hiding place and called to the breeze to come and cool him: *"Aura! Aura!"* Procris, thinking that it was the name of a mistress, jumped up from her hiding place. Hearing her, and supposing the sound to be that of an animal, Cephalus cast his unerring spear and killed Procris.

The third daughter, Orithyia, was snatched away from the banks of the Ilissus River by Boreas, the god of the north wind. He carried his bride off to Thrace, where they had two winged sons, Zetes and Calais, who became **Argonauts** (*Outward voyage*), and a daughter, Cleopatra, who married Phineus. Cleopatra and Phineus had two sons. On Cleopatra's death, Phineus married Idaea, who, in anger at her stepsons (sometimes the cause of her anger is said to have been their rejection of her amorous overtures), accused them to Phineus of improper advances to her. Phineus put out their eyes and imprisoned them in a cave. Phineus' punishment for this is mentioned in the story of the **Argonauts** (*Outward voyage*).

Ion was the next king of Athens, and then came a second Cecrops, followed by a second Pandion. (Such duplications were often made in order to fit some ancient annalist's chronological scheme.) This Pandion had several sons, including Aegeus and Nisus. Aegeus became king of Athens, Nisus of Megara.

While Nisus was king of Megara, his land was invaded by Minos of Crete. The daughter of Nisus, Scylla, fell in love with the invader Minos, and to gain his love betrayed her father, by snipping off a magic lock of purple hair which rendered him and his city impregnable so long as it grew on his head. Scylla took the purple lock to Minos, and Megara at once fell to him. But Minos refused to have anything to do with the treacherous Scylla. He sailed away homeward, and Scylla plunged into the sea and clung to the stern of his ship. As she clung, she was transformed into a sea bird. Nisus became a sea eagle, which constantly pursued the sea bird. (Compare the similar story of Amphitryon, Comaetho, and Pterelaus, under **Heracles,** *Background*).

For Aegeus, see **Theseus,** his son and the greatest of all the Athenian heroes.

Of the Athenian stories, the favorite with poets has always been that of Philomela, Procne, and Tereus. Ovid has it in the *Metamorphoses,* 6, Chaucer in *The Legend of Good Women;* it permeates Shakespeare's *Titus Andronicus;* Matthew Arnold wrote a *Philomela* (1853), Swinburne an *Itylus* (1866); T. S. Eliot uses the theme in *The Waste Land* (1922). Also worthy of mention are Euripides' *Ion,* Ovid's telling of the story of Procris and Cephalus (*Metamorphoses,* 7), and Swinburne's *Erechtheus* (1876).

Atlas was a giant who held the sky on his shoulders. He was turned to stone by **Perseus.** See also **Heracles** (eleventh Labor).

Atreus (ā'trūs), king of Mycenae, and Thyestes were sons of **Pelops,** under whose name are described the earlier family history and the curse that was inherited. As a result of the family curse, the brothers were at odds, and the results of their quarreling form the beginning of the story that has been the most fruitful of all mythological sources for tragic drama. Ever so many variant details have crept into the story over the ages; here only the chief and most canonical points can be included.

Thyestes seduced Aerope, wife of Atreus, or he stole from the flock of Atreus a golden ram (or both). The revenge of Atreus was terrible: pretending forgiveness, he invited Thyestes to a banquet, and there served to him the cooked limbs of Thyestes' slaughtered children, revealing the nature of the meal after Thyestes had eaten. Thyestes' revenge was grim. By incest with his own daughter Pelopia, he begot a son Aegisthus who murdered Atreus. Thyestes now succeeded to the throne of Mycenae, and at his death Agamemnon, son of Atreus (though sometimes a Pleisthenes, son of Atreus and father of Agamemnon and Menelaus, creeps into the genealogy), became king. While Agamemnon was away at the siege of Troy, Aegisthus became the lover of Clytemnestra, wife of Agamemnon. Both Aegisthus and

Clytemnestra wanted revenge on Agamemnon, he because of Thyestes' "banquet," she because of the sacrifice of Iphigenia at Aulis (see under **Trojan War,** *Rallying of the host*). On Agamemnon's return, Clytemnestra and Aegisthus murdered him in his bath, and murdered also Cassandra, the Trojan princess whom he had brought home as his concubine. Aegisthus became king of Mycenae.

At the time of the murder, Orestes, the young son of Agamemnon, was hustled away to safety by his sister, Electra. Orestes grew up in exile, at the court of King Strophius of Phocis, where he and the son of Strophius, Pylades, became inseparable friends. Meanwhile, at home, Electra was treated as a slave, because of her hatred of the murderers and her loyalty to her father's memory; another sister, Chrysothemis, capitulated and lived at ease with her mother and Aegisthus. Grown to manhood, Orestes returns, accompanied by Pylades and backed by the oracle of Apollo at Delphi, to take revenge and regain the throne. After establishing contact with Electra, Orestes, aided by her and Pylades, kills Aegisthus and Clytemnestra. For the latter act he is pursued by the Furies (for whom see under **Hades,** *Underworld*). He seeks refuge at Delphi, is purified by Apollo, but told that he must be tried for murder before the court of the Areopagus in Athens. He goes to Athens, and the trial takes place. The Furies are the prosecutors, Apollo speaks in Orestes' defense, Athena presides. The citizens of Athens vote, and when the vote is a tie, Athena casts her ballot for acquittal.

The curse of the house of Atreus is now pretty much at an end, but there are further adventures of Orestes. The best known is that in which he is unable to escape the fits of madness sent upon him by the Furies until he goes with Pylades, at the bidding of Apollo, to the far-off land of the Taurians (probably the Crimea) to bring back "the sister." Orestes thinks this means a statue of Apollo's sister Artemis. But in the land of the Taurians, Orestes' sister, Iphigenia, saved by Artemis at the moment of sacrifice at Aulis, is the priestess of a savage cult of Artemis, in which all strangers to the land are sacrificed to the goddess. Orestes and Pylades are caught and are about to be sacrificed when a recognition between sister and brother is effected. All escape from King Thoas and the Taurians and bring with them the cult statue of Artemis, thus bringing back two sisters. Pylades and Electra marry. Orestes marries his cousin Hermione, daughter of Helen and Menelaus. Hermione's hand is also claimed by Neoptolemus, son of Achilles, and in a quarrel over her Neoptolemus is killed at Delphi, by Orestes. Orestes and Hermione had one child, Tisamenus, who became king of Sparta. Orestes eventually died of a snake bite.

The house of Atreus has been a rich quarry for tragic poets. Space permits the listing of only a few of the many important plays on the theme: Aeschylus, *Agamemnon, Choephoroi, Eumenides;* Sophocles, *Electra;* Euripides, *Electra, Iphigenia among the Taurians;* Seneca, *Thyestes,*

Agamemnon; Alfieri, *Agamemnon, Orestes* (both 1777); Goethe, *Iphigenie auf Tauris* (1787); Hofmannsthal, *Elektra* (1903); Robinson Jeffers, *Tower beyond Tragedy* (1925); O'Neill, *Mourning Becomes Electra* (1931); Giraudoux, *Electre* (1937); T. S. Eliot, *The Family Reunion* (1939); Sartre, *Les Mouches* (1943), English translation, *The Flies* (1948).

Atrides (a-trī'dēz) means son of **Atreus,** and refers to Agamemnon or Menelaus.

Atropos (at'rō-pos) was one of the **Fates.**

Augeas (aw-jē'as) was the king of Elis whose stable **Heracles** cleansed (sixth Labor).

Aulis (aw'lis) is the place from which the Greek fleet set sail, on the second attempt, to Troy. See **Trojan War** (*Rallying of the host*).

Aurora (aw-ror'a) is Eos, the dawn goddess. See **Sky Deities.**

Auster (aws'ter) is Notus, the south wind. See **Wind Deities.**

Autolycus (aw-tol'i-kus) was a son of **Hermes.**

Bacchus (bak'us) is a name of **Dionysus.**

Battus was punished by **Hermes** for betraying him.

Baucis (baw'sis) was the wife of **Philemon.**

Bellerophon (be-lĕr'ō-fon) was a descendant of Sisyphus, the founder of Corinth. While Bellerophon was on a visit at the court of King Proetus of Argus, the wife of Proetus, Stheneboea (or Anteia), attempted to seduce him, and when the attempt failed, alleged to Proetus that the young Bellerophon had made unseemly advances to her. Proetus consequently sent Bellerophon away to the kingdom of his son-in-law, Iobates of Lycia, and sent with him a message bidding Iobates do away with the bearer. There followed a series of exploits or tests, imposed on Bellerophon by Iobates, the first and most famous being against the creature known as the Chimaera, a threefold beast, part lion, part goat, and part dragon, which laid waste the fields of Lycia. With the help of the winged horse Pegasus, Bellerophon slew the Chimaera.

Pegasus requires a brief digression. He was the offspring of Medusa by Poseidon (see under **Sea Deities**), and in some stories was the bearer of Zeus's thunderbolts. He is said to have started the famous spring called

Hippocrene, on Mount Helicon in Boeotia, by striking the mountain top with his hoof. Hippocrene and Helicon were always associated with the Muses and with poetic inspiration. Bellerophon was aided by Athena in taming Pegasus. She showed the hero in a vision where he could find a golden bridle that would subdue the steed. Bellerophon caught and bridled Pegasus at Pirene, the fountain of Corinth.

Bellerophon's other tasks are less well known. He conquered the Solymi, a fierce but obscure tribe in Asia Minor, and had an encounter, presumably successful, with the Amazons. Finally, he defeated and killed a band of Lycian warriors sent by Iobates to ambush him. Thereupon Iobates recognized the merits of Bellerophon, gave him his daughter in marriage, and made him heir to half his kingdom. But the story does not end at this successful point. Later, Bellerophon, mounted on Pegasus, tried to fly to heaven. Pegasus reached heaven, but Bellerophon was thrown off, was injured in the fall, and ended his life a lame and lonely wanderer, "Maimed, beggared, grey; seeking an alms," as he is described in George Meredith's *Bellerophon* (1887). Two stories in *The Earthly Paradise* (1868–1870), by William Morris, are about Bellerophon: *Bellerophon at Argos* and *Bellerophon in Lycia*.

Bellona (be-lō′na) was a Roman goddess of war.

Boreas (bō′rē-as) is the north wind. See **Wind Deities.**

Briareus (brī-ā′rē-us) was one of the hundred-handed giants, sons of **Earth and Sky.**

Briseis (brī-sē′is) was a young woman, a prize of war taken from Achilles by Agamemnon in the **Trojan War** (*Iliad*).

Britomartis (brī-tō-mar′tis) was a nymph of **Artemis.**

* **Bromius** (brō′mi-us) is an epithet of **Dionysus.**

† **Brontes** (bron′tēz) was one of the Cyclopes, sons of **Earth and Sky.**

The **Bronze Age** was the third of the **Ages of Man.**

Busiris (bū-sī′ris) was an Egyptian king encountered by **Heracles** (*Minor stories*).

The **Cabiri** (ka-bī′rī) were the deities of a mystery religion centered in the island of Samothrace.

*read: (brō′mi-us), literally "noisy,"   †read: (bron′tēz), the thunderer,

Cacus (kā′kus) was a giant who stole Geryon's cattle from **Heracles** (tenth Labor).

Cadmus (kad′mus) was the founder of **Thebes.**

The **Caduceus** (ka-dū′shus) is the messenger's wand of **Hermes.** *

Caeneus (sē′nūs), a Lapith of Thessaly, was once a girl, beloved of Poseidon, changed, at her own request, to a man, and made invulnerable. Caeneus met his end by being buried under pine trees by the centaurs, during the battle of the Lapiths and the centaurs.

Calchas (kal′kas) was the leading seer of the Greeks in the Trojan War.

Calliope (ka-lī′ō-pē) was one of the nine **Muses,** patroness of epic poetry.

Callisto (ka-lis′tō) was a nymph and follower of **Artemis.**

The **Calydonian** (ka-li-dō′ni-an) **Boar Hunt** is the fourth in importance of the great incidents and heroic rallying points of Greek myth, after the stories of Troy, Thebes, and the Argonauts. Oeneus, king of Calydon, in Aetolia, in western Greece, forgot to offer sacrifice to Artemis when sacrificing to the gods. In anger, Artemis sent a huge wild boar that damaged the property and the persons of the Calydonians. A hunt was organized under the leadership of the king's son, Meleager. Here a digression is necessary: at the birth of Meleager, his mother, Althea, was warned that her son's life would last only as long as it took a certain brand, then burning on the hearth before her, to be consumed by fire. Althea snatched the brand from the fire and hid it away. Meleager grew to robust young manhood.

All the great heroes of the age were present for the hunt: Castor and Polydeuces; Jason of the Argonauts; Theseus of Athens and his friend Pirithous; Peleus, father of Achilles, and Telamon, father of Ajax; Amphiaraus of the Seven against Thebes; Admetus, husband of Alcestis. A very special person was Atalanta, peerless huntress from Arcadia. (Whether this maiden is the same as the **Atalanta** of the bridal race is uncertain; for that story, see under her name.) The two brothers of Althea, Toxeus and Plexippus, sons of Thestius, were also there. Meleager was in love with Atalanta, and in spite of the grumbling of some of the heroes against the participation of a woman, insisted that she be permitted to join in the hunt. The hunt took its course; dogs and even men perished beneath the great beast's tusks. Peleus' spearcast was wild, and struck and killed another hunter, Eurytion. Atalanta struck the boar the first blow, in its back; then Amphiaraus lodged a spear in its eye, and finally Meleager dealt it a death blow. A quarrel arose over the spoils. Meleager insisted on giving them (the head and hide

*read: (ka-dū′sē-us)

of the animal) to Atalanta, because she scored the first hit. His uncles, Toxeus and Plexippus, objected violently, and in the mêlée that followed Meleager killed them both. The news was brought to Althea. In sisterly sorrow and anger she went to the hiding place of the fatal brand, took it out, and threw it into the fire. As it was consumed, Meleager, far out on the plain, drooped in death. Althea took her own life.

There is a different version of this story in the *Iliad,* with no magic brand and no Atalanta. It was the men of Calydon and their neighbors the Curetes who hunted the boar in this version. In a dispute over the spoils of honor, Meleager killed his uncle, the leader of the Curetes. The Curetes invaded Calydon; Althea cursed her son. In anger, Meleager refused to fight, staying at home with his lovely bride, Cleopatra. The Curetes stormed the city; Oeneus, the men of Calydon, and even Althea pleaded with Meleager to fight, offering him great rewards, but he refused. At last, with the city on fire, Cleopatra begged him to go out. Then he did so, and repelled the Curetes. But because he had delayed, he no longer got the rich gifts he had once been offered.

The familiar version is in Ovid's *Metamorphoses,* 8. Swinburne's long lyrical drama, *Atalanta in Calydon* (1865), is probably his best major poem.

Calypso (ka-lip'sō) was a nymph who held **Odysseus** (*Sea adventures*) prisoner on her island.

Camilla (ka-mil'a) was a maiden warrior in the alliance in Italy against **Aeneas.**

Capaneus (kap'a-nūs) was one of the Seven against **Thebes.**

Cassandra (ka-san'dra), daughter of Priam, was a prophetess whom no one believed. See **Apollo** and **Trojan War.**

Cassiopeia (ka-si-ō-pē'a) was the mother of Andromeda. See **Perseus.**

Castalia (kas-tā'li-a), a spring on Mount Parnassus, near Delphi, was a haunt of the Muses.

Castor (kas'tor) and Polydeuces were the twin sons of **Leda** and Zeus.

Cecrops (sē'krops) was an early king of **Athens.**

Celaeno (se-lē'nō) was one of the Harpies. See **Aeneas** (*Wanderings*) and **Sea Deities.**

The **Centaurs** (sen'tawrz) were mostly equine, but with the head, arms, and breast of a human being; they had four horse's legs, a horse's body and tail.

They were for the most part a wild, boisterous, and lascivious tribe, and liable to start riots, especially when drunk. For their wild behavior at the wedding of Pirithous, king of the Lapiths, see under **Theseus** (*Later adventures*). The centaurs lived in Thessaly, in the north of ancient Greece, and were reputed to be descended from Ixion and a cloud. The good centaur, Chiron, was unlike the rest. Son of Cronus and the nymph Philyra, he alone was immortal. He was gentle and wise, skilled in music, hunting, and medical lore, and was the tutor of various great figures, including Achilles, Jason, and Asclepius. In art Chiron is often represented with human front legs. His wife was the nymph Chariclo, and their daughters, apparently human in form, were Endeis, wife of **Aeacus,** and Ocyrhoe. Ovid tells of Ocyrhoe's powers of prophecy and her transformation into a mare. For the willing surrender of immortality by Chiron, see under **Heracles** (third Labor).

Cephalus (sef'a-lus) was beloved of Eos (see **Sky Deities**) and husband of Procris (see **Athens**).

Cerberus (sur'bur-us) was the three-headed dog of the underworld. See **Hades**.

Ceres (sē'rēz) is the Roman name of **Demeter**.

The **Cerynaean** (ser-i-nē'an) **Hind** was caught by **Heracles** (fourth Labor).

Ceyx (sē'ix) was the husband of **Alcyone**.

Chaos (kā'os) is, according to Hesiod, the first thing that came to be. Never more than just a vague and vaguely located (sometimes in the underworld) concept of primeval matter, Chaos nevertheless is the progenitor of certain beings. Its direct offspring are Erebus (Darkness), which is sometimes a region of the underworld, and Night. Night was the mother, and Erebus the father, of Day and Aether (the clear, thin upper air, sometimes supposed to be fiery). Night, by herself or by unknown fathers, gave birth to numerous abstractions of some interest: Nemesis (Righteous Indignation), Death, Sleep, Eris (the goddess of strife), the **Fates** (who, however, are also said to be daughters of Zeus and Themis), and the Hesperides (for whom see **Heracles,** eleventh Labor). Eris bore Lethe (Forgetfulness, often one of the rivers of the underworld, for which see **Hades**), and various unpleasant concepts, including Toil, Hunger, Quarrels, and Sorrows. There are other abstract children of Night too. With a few exceptions, such as the Fates, this breed of Chaos is mythologically insignificant.

The **Charites** (kar'i-tēz) are the three Graces, daughters of Zeus and Eurynome. They are the personification of gracefulness. The singular is Charis (ka'ris). Their names (usually) are Aglaia, Euphrosyne, and Thalia.

Charon (kā'ron) was the boatman who ferried the souls of the dead to the underworld. See **Hades.**

Charybdis (ka-rib'dis), a sea monster resembling a whirlpool, was encountered by Odysseus.

The **Chimaera** (kī-mē'ra) was a monster, part lion, part goat, and part snake. See **Bellerophon.**

Chiron (ki'ron) was the one wise and gentle creature among the **Centaurs.**

Chloris (klor'is), wife of Zephyrus, the west wind, was goddess of flowers.

Chrysaor (kri-sā'or) was the son of Medusa and Poseidon. See **Sea Deities.**

Chryseis (krī-sē'is) was a maiden restored by Agamemnon to her father, a priest of Apollo, in the Trojan War.

Chrysothemis (kri-soth'e-mis) was the sister of Electra and Orestes. See **Atreus.**

The **Cicones** (si-kō'nēz) were a Thracian people whom **Odysseus** (*Sea adventures*) raided.

The **Cimmerians** (si-mē'ri-anz) lived in mist and darkness in the far west. **Odysseus** (*Sea adventures*) visited them.

Cinyras (sin'i-ras), king of Cyprus, had a daughter, Myrrha. Myrrha was cursed with an uncontrollable passion for her father, and by a trick shared his bed night after night, while Cinyras thought that his mistress was another girl. At length Cinyras discovered the truth, and his shame and anger were so terrible that he threatened Myrrha with a sword, and when she fled killed himself. Myrrha lived a life of anguish, and at last was turned into a myrrh tree, with ever-flowing tears of gum. From the myrrh tree was born Adonis, whom **Aphrodite** loved. The story of Cinyras and Myrrha is told in Ovid's *Metamorphoses,* 10.

Circe (sur'sē) was a famous witch encountered by **Odysseus** (*Sea adventures*).

Cithaeron (si-thē'ron) is the mountain where Oedipus of **Thebes** was exposed as a child.

Cleopatra (klē-ō-pat'ra) was (1) wife of Meleager in one version of the **Calydonian Boar Hunt**; (2) daughter of Boreas and Orithyia and wife of Phineus (see **Athens**).

Clio (klī'ō) was one of the nine **Muses,** patroness of history.

Clotho (klō'thō) was one of the three **Fates.**

Clymene (klim'e-nē) was mother of Phaethon by the sun god. See **Sky Deities.**

Clytemnestra (klī-tem-nes'tra) was the wife of Agamemnon, son of **Atreus.**

Cocytus (ko-sī'tus) was one of the rivers of the underworld. See **Hades** (*Underworld*).

Coeus (sē'us) was one of the **Titans.**

Colchis (kol'kis) is the land of the Golden Fleece sought by the **Argonauts.**

Colonus (ko-lō'nus) was a region near Athens, where Oedipus of **Thebes** ended his life.

Cora (ko'ra), or **Core** (ko'rē), or **Kore,** means "the maiden" and refers to Persephone. See **Hades.**

Coronis (ko-rō'nis) was the mother of Asclepius by **Apollo.**

The **Corybantes** (kor-i-ban'tēz) were attendants of Cybele. See **Mother-Goddesses.**

Cottus (kot'us) was one of the three hundred-handed giants, sons of **Earth and Sky.**

Creon (krē'on) was (1) a king of **Thebes** (*Antigone*); (2) a king of Corinth (see **Argonauts**). *

Cresphontes (kres-fon'tēz) was the husband of Merope. See the end of the article **Heracles.**

Cressida (kres'i-da) belongs to medieval, not ancient, myth. She is the mistress of Troilus in the medieval love story that was attached to the story of Troy. Her name comes from Chryseis. See **Trojan War** (*Early events*).

Crete, the largest of the Aegean islands, was the place of origin and the center of the Minoan civilization, which reached a high level of social and artistic development early in the second millennium B.C. From this early culture the Greeks, invading from the north, took over much of what contributed to the flowering of Hellenic civilization. Crete is important not only in Aegean civilization but also in Greek mythology.

*add: The name Creon means "ruler."

Agenor, king of Tyre, had a son Cadmus (for whom see **Thebes**) and a daughter Europa. While Europa was playing one day on the seashore with her maiden companions, Zeus, smitten by love for her, appeared before her in the form of a gentle, snow-white bull. He induced Europa to seat herself upon him, and at once swam away through the sea, with Europa on his back. He swam to Crete, resumed his proper form, and begot three sons by Europa. These were Minos, king of Crete, Rhadamanthus, king of the lesser islands, and Sarpedon, who founded a dynasty in Lycia. Both Minos and Rhadamanthus became judges of the underworld after their death. Minos figures as a minor character in many stories (see especially under **Athens** and **Theseus,** *Minotaur*). He and his wife Pasiphae, daughter of Helius, the sun god, had as children Ariadne, Phaedra, and Androgeus, for whom see under **Theseus** (*Minotaur; Hippolytus*). Pasiphae is said to have become enamored of a bull, by whom she gave birth to the monstrous Minotaur (see **Theseus**). Daedalus, the builder of the Labyrinth, in which the Minotaur was housed, is said to have built also a wooden cow, within which Pasiphae satisfied her unnatural passion. Daedalus was an Athenian, but had been exiled for the murder of his nephew Talus (or Perdix), who was his rival as a master craftsman. Talus had invented the saw, and Daedalus murdered him out of envy. After building the Labyrinth, Daedalus was held prisoner on Crete, by Minos. At last he built wings, to enable himself and his son, Icarus, to escape. He fastened them to their shoulders by means of wax, and warned Icarus not to fly too high, lest the heat of the sun melt the wax, nor too low, lest the wings be dampened by the sea. At first the flight was a great success, but then Icarus, exulting in the experience, soared aloft. The wax melted and the boy fell into the sea and was drowned. The area where he fell is the Icarian Sea, named for him. Daedalus made his escape, and went to Sicily. Thither he was pursued by Minos, but a certain King Cocalus protected him and brought about the death of Minos. Ovid's *Metamorphoses* has the story of Europa (Book 2) and of Daedalus' flight (Book 8).

Creusa (krē-ū′sa) was (1) the wife of **Aeneas,** lost in the flight from Troy; (2) a princess of Corinth (see **Argonauts**); (3) a daughter of Erechtheus of **Athens.**

Cronus (krō′nus), Roman Saturn, chief of the **Titans,** son of **Earth and Sky,** was husband of his sister Rhea and, by her, father of Hestia, Demeter, Hera, Pluto, Poseidon, and Zeus. The story of the birth of Cronus's children is told under **Zeus.** Uranus, the Sky, hated his own children, and hid them away as soon as they were born, in hollow places of Earth. Mother Earth, in distress, urged her children to punish Sky, and Cronus, the youngest born, took the curved knife that his mother offered and with it cut off the genital organs of his father, thus separating Sky from Earth. Cronus threw the severed organs into the sea. From drops of blood that fell from them to the ground sprang the Furies (see under **Hades**), the Giants (see under **Zeus**), and certain nymphs called the Meliae. From the genital organs, as they gathered foam (*aphros*) in the sea, was born Aphrodite.

Cronus was now supreme ruler, and in the period of his rule men lived without sorrow, sickness, or old age. They did not work, for the land produced abundance without toil. Death came gently, and men remained on earth as beneficent spirits. See further under the **Ages of Man.** Cronus is sometimes said to be father of Chiron the centaur, by the ocean nymph Philyra.

Cupid is the Roman name for **Eros.**

The **Curetes** (kū-rē'tēz) were (1) warriors who protected the infant **Zeus;** (2) warriors in the Homeric version of the **Calydonian Boar Hunt.**

Cybele (sib'e-lē) was a Phrygian **Mother-Goddess.**

The **Cyclops** (sī'klops) was (1) a one-eyed giant encountered by **Odysseus** (*Sea adventures*); (2) one of three Cyclopes (sī-klō'pēz), divine metalworkers, sons of **Earth and Sky.**

Cydippe (sī-dip'ē) was beloved of **Acontius.**

Cyllene (si-le'ne) is a mountain in Arcadia, where Hermes was born.

Cynthia (sin'thi-a) is an epithet of Artemis, from **Cynthus.**

Cynthius (sin'thi-us) is an epithet of Apollo, from **Cynthus.**

Cynthus (sin'thus) is a hill on the island of Delos, birthplace of **Apollo** and **Artemis.**

Cypris (sī'pris) is a name of Aphrodite, from the island of Cyprus, a center of her worship.

Cyrene (sī-rē'nē) was a nymph whom **Apollo** loved, and the eponym of the Libyan city of Cyrene.

Cytherea (sith-e-rē'a) is a name of Aphrodite, from the island of Cythera, a center of her worship.

Daedalus (dē'da-lus) was the builder of the Labyrinth and the first flier. See **Crete.**

Danae (da'na-ē) was the mother of **Perseus** by Zeus.

The **Danaids** (dan'ā-idz) were the fifty daughters of Danaus. Their descent from **Io** can most easily be shown by a chart:

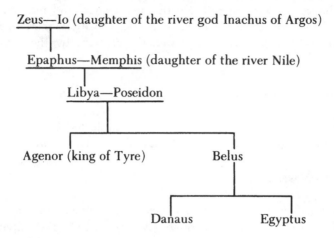

Zeus—Io (daughter of the river god Inachus of Argos)

Epaphus—Memphis (daughter of the river Nile)

Libya—Poseidon

Agenor (king of Tyre)   Belus

Danaus   Egyptus

Danaus with his fifty daughters, and his brother Egyptus, who had fifty sons, lived in Egypt. But the brothers quarreled, and Danaus fled with his fifty daughters to their ancestral home of Argos. Egyptus and his sons pursued them there, intent on marriage between the cousins. Though opposing the multiple match, Danaus pretended to agree to it. But he gave his daughters swords and bade them kill their bridegrooms on their wedding night. Forty-nine of them did so; for their punishment for this murder, see under **Hades** (*Underworld*). One spared her husband, because she loved him. This was Hypermnestra, who is called by Horace *splendide mendax*. She and her husband Lynceus were the progenitors of the rulers of Argos; among their descendants were Perseus and Heracles. Part of the story was used by Aeschylus in *The Suppliants;* Chaucer has Hypermnestra in *The Legend of Good Women*.

Danaus (dan'ā-us) was the father of the **Danaids.**

Daphne (daf'nē) was beloved of **Apollo** and became a laurel tree.

Dardanus (dar'da-nus) was a son of Zeus and founder of Troy.

Deianira (dē-ya-ni'ra) was the second wife of **Heracles** and caused his death.

Deidamia (dē-i-da-mi'a) was the mother of Neoptolemus by Achilles.

Deiphobus (dē-if'ō-bus), son of Priam, fought in the **Trojan War** (*The fall*).

Delia (dē'li-a) is an epithet of Artemis and

Delius (dē'li-us) an epithet of Apollo; both are from

Delos (dē'los), the Aegean island where they were born.

Delphi (del'fi), on the side of Mount Parnassus in central Greece, is the site of **Apollo's** great oracle.

Demeter (dē-mē'ter), Roman Ceres, daughter of Cronus and Rhea, and elder sister of Zeus, is the goddess of grain, the sponsor of the growth of the crops. She is represented as a mature and dignified woman. Much the best-known story about her is her part in the incident of the abduction by Hades of her daughter Persephone, told under **Hades** (*Persephone*). Demeter is the mother also of Plutus, god of wealth, a negligible figure in myth, as is his father Iasion. For the identity of Plutus and Pluto, see under **Hades.** The curious little story of Erysichthon of Thessaly is also connected with Demeter. He chopped down a tree in a grove sacred to Demeter, and was punished by her with insatiable hunger. Eventually the unlucky man began to eat himself and so died.

Demodocus (dē-mod'ō-kus) was a minstrel at the court of Alcinous, visited by **Odysseus** (*Sea adventures*).

Demophoon (dē-mof'ō-on) was the son of King Celeus of Eleusis. See **Hades** (*Persephone*).

Deucalion (dū-kā'li-on) is the Greek Noah. He and his wife Pyrrha are the principal figures in the Greek flood story. He was son of Prometheus; Pyrrha was daughter of Prometheus' brother Epimetheus. This was in the early days of mankind, and Zeus was displeased by the behavior of the majority of men. When King Lycaon of Arcadia went so far as to offer human flesh as a banquet for the gods, simply to test their omniscience, Zeus resolved to do away with man. And so, having turned Lycaon into a wolf, he inundated the world. Deucalion and Pyrrha, forewarned by Prometheus, built themselves a raft and floated above the destruction, the only survivors of the flood. After many days they came to rest on top of Mount Parnassus. As the waters receded, they made their way to the oracle of Themis (later to be the oracle of Apollo) and there asked how they could repeople the earth. The response was, as oracular responses so often are, puzzling. They were told to throw their mother's bones over their shoulders. At last Deucalion reasoned that the mother of all is Ge (Earth), and that her bones are the stones. Every stone that Deucalion threw behind him sprang up as a man; every one that Pyrrha threw became a woman. It is from this origin, says Ovid in his version of the story (*Metamorphoses*, 1), that man derives his flinty nature.

Quite apart from this unique kind of procreation, Deucalion and Pyrrha are in another way the progenitors of many of the Greeks. They had a son, Hellen, the eponym of the Hellenes (as the Greeks called and still call themselves). Hellen had three sons, Dorus, Aeolus, and Xuthus. Xuthus had two sons, Ion and Achaeus. The four great racial divisions that the ancient Greeks made among themselves were the Dorians, the Aeolians, the Ionians, and the Achaeans. The children of **Aeolus** are also an important mythical family.

Diana (dī-an′a) is the Roman name of **Artemis.**

Dictynna (dik-tin′a) was a nymph of **Artemis.**

Dido (dī′dō) was the founder and queen of Carthage. See **Aeneas** (*Wanderings*).

Diomedes (dī-ō-mē′dēz), or Diomed, was (1) a prominent Greek warrior in the **Trojan War** (*Iliad*); (2) a Thracian king whose horses **Heracles** took (eighth Labor).

Dione (dī-ō′nē) was a wife of **Zeus.**

Dionysus (dī-ō-nī′sus), whom the Romans usually called Bacchus, though this too is a Greek name, is the son of Zeus and Semele. He is the god of wine, and, in Greek stories, of much more besides: he represents the surge and excitement of life and growth, and the intoxication not only of wine but of animal impulse. He usually appears as a rather effeminate-seeming youth, with soft face and flowing hair, perhaps carrying a thyrsus (a staff tipped with a pine cone and wreathed with ribbons or vine leaves), often attended by his band of followers, called the thiasus. He is called Liber, Bromius, Lyaeus (all connected with his powers), and is sometimes identified in story with Iacchus, a minor deity of the Eleusinian mysteries, for which see **Hades** (*Persephone*).

Semele was a Theban princess, daughter of Cadmus. Zeus was her lover. In jealousy, Hera came to Semele disguised as a crone, hinted that her lover was not Zeus, but an impostor, and urged the girl to make him prove his identity by coming to her in all his radiant divinity. Zeus unwillingly did so (Semele had made him swear to fulfill any promise she might exact) and Semele was burned to death by his brilliance. Her unborn child was saved by Zeus and sewn up in his thigh, to be born again from there when ripe for birth. The child was Dionysus. Hermes took him from Zeus at birth and gave him first to Ino, Semele's sister, to nurse, and then to certain nymphs of Nysa, in Asia Minor. Silenus too is sometimes said to have been the nurse of Dionysus. His youth was spent in wandering; at one time he was driven mad by Hera and cured by Rhea Cybele; he wandered to India and learned Eastern wisdom; eventually he returned to Greece and introduced the culture of the vine and the making of wine, which he had learned or invented during his travels.

He is regularly surrounded by the devoted and often frenzied thiasus. This group consists of female followers called maenads and nymphs, who are of normal female appearance, though the nymphs are minor deities rather than ordinary mortal women, and male followers called satyrs and sileni, who are not of normal male appearance. There is no consistent difference between a satyr and a silenus; both are sometimes represented as being men with horse's tails and ears, sometimes as men with the tails, hind hoofs, and sometimes a few other appurtenances, of goats. Often the sileni are represented as being somewhat more serious and older than the satyrs, and Silenus, who is merely a collective singular of his race, is nurse and even tutor of Dionysus. Both species drink much and pursue the nymphs and maenads in a perpetual state of sexual excitement. The nymphs and maenads nurse wild animals, or, in a different mood, they may rend them with their bare hands. Miracles such as the springing up of fountains of milk and wine and prodigious feats of strength are common features of the thiasus. Music and dancing are usual.

Dionysus is patron of music and the arts, especially of the drama and of the dithyramb, a choral song-and-dance performance; he is sometimes called Dithyrambus. Patronage of the arts is one point of contact with Apollo; another is the fact that Dionysus was connected with Delphi, and was thought of as an alternate resident of the shrine, while Apollo was away.

Most stories of Dionysus have to do with his worship, and the punishment of those who oppose it. There is very little romance in his career; his one love was Ariadne, whom he found on Naxos after Theseus had abandoned her. None of their four sons is of mythological interest. There is an obscure story wherein he is father of Deianira (wife of Heracles) by Althea, wife of Oeneus of Calydon; Oeneus is said to have been the first man to receive a vine plant from the god.

Two stories of Dionysus' revenge are well known, those of Lycurgus and of Pentheus. Lycurgus expelled the god and imprisoned his thiasus. Dionysus returned, freed his worshipers, and caused Lycurgus to go mad. Thereafter Lycurgus was either imprisoned, or caused by his own subjects to be torn to pieces by wild horses. (Tearing to pieces is the usual form of death of the foes of Dionysus, and probably has its origins in a religious ritual; note that Dionysus himself is, according to Orphic tradition [see **Orpheus**], torn to pieces by the Titans.) Pentheus is a more famous victim, thanks to Euripides' great play, *The Bacchae*, which tells the story. Pentheus, king of Thebes, son of Agave, grandson of Cadmus, cousin of Dionysus, seeks to prevent the women of Thebes from joining the god's thiasus (it is usually the women who are ready to accept Dionysus and join in the emotional frenzy of his worship), and throws into prison a mysterious "priest" of Dionysus. The prisoner (who is the god himself) miraculously escapes and mesmerizes Pentheus into spying on the women as they celebrate the rites of the god in the fields. Dionysus reveals the presence of the king, and in the madness of their Dionysiac frenzy the women tear him to pieces, believing him to be a wild animal. Agave triumphantly carries back to Thebes her son's head, and only later returns to sanity and grief.

Sometimes women refuse to join the god's worship, and suffer for it. Thus the daughters of King Proetus of Tiryns would not accept the god's rites and went mad, until the famous seer Melampus cured them by the psychiatric technique of channeling their frenzy into wild dancing, whereby they recovered sanity. The daughters of King Minyas of Orchomenus in Boeotia likewise declined to worship the god, and sat at home weaving. Dionysus, disguised as a maiden, came to them and urged them to join. When they still refused, the room filled with strange music and scent, vines sprang up, and the young women went mad. In some versions they are said to have torn to pieces the son of one of them, and the usual ending is that all of them are transformed into bats.

When pirates attempted to kidnap Dionysus, his revenge was relatively mild. Again music, vines, and scents filled the air; the wicked crew threw themselves from the ship, and were turned into dolphins.

The story of Icarius and Erigone is of a different sort. Icarius lived in Attica in the early days. He was hospitable to Dionysus, and in return was taught how to make wine. But when Icarius gave his neighbors some of his new beverage, they thought they were poisoned and killed Icarius. His daughter Erigone knew nothing of her father's death, and searched everywhere for him. When at last she found him dead she hanged herself for grief. A drought ensued, which was not dispelled until at Dionysus' insistence a ceremony commemorating the death of Icarius and Erigone was instituted. Here once more some sort of religious ritual seems to lie behind the story.

There were, especially in late antiquity, religious rites connected with Dionysus analogous to the Eleusinian Mysteries (see *Persephone*, under **Hades**) and the Orphic religious ideas. In fact, Orpheus is said to have "invented" the mysteries of Dionysus. Semele, though usually a mortal woman, is sometimes said to have been brought up from the underworld by Dionysus, to have been renamed Tyone, and then to have gone up to heaven with her son.

The **Dioscuri** (dī-os-cū′rī) were Castor and Polydeuces, sons of Zeus and **Leda**.

Dirce (dur′sē) was punished by Amphion and Zethus of **Thebes**.

Dis (dis) is a Roman name of **Hades**.

Dodona (dō-dō′na) is the site of an oracle of Zeus in northwestern Greece.

Dolon (dō′lon) was a Trojan spy caught by Diomedes and Odysseus in the **Trojan War** (*Iliad*).

Doris (dor′is) was the wife of Nereus. Both were **Sea Deities.**

Dryades (dri′a-dēz), or Dryads, were tree **nymphs.**

Dryope (dri′ō-pē) was turned into a tree **nymph.**

Earth and Sky. In Hesiod's *Theogony*, which is the nearest thing to a canonical account of origins, Mother Earth (Ge, Gaea, Tellus) is without parents, primeval, second in antiquity to Chaos only: "At first Chaos came into being, but then Earth, the broad-bosomed." Earth of herself bore Sky (Uranus), the Mountains, and Pontus the Sea. From the union of Earth and Sky are descended nearly all the major deities of myth. Their most celebrated offspring are the twelve Titans, who are in their turn ancestors of most of the chief gods. The story of the revolt of the Titans under Cronus against their father is told under **Cronus.** There are two other sets of children of Earth and Sky. The Cyclopes, three one-eyed creatures who manufacture the thunderbolts of Zeus, are one group; their names are Brontes (the Thunderer), Steropes (the Flasher), and Arges (the Bright One). (The Cyclopes whom **Odysseus,** *Sea adventures,* encounters are different, though also one-eyed. They are pastoral dwellers, not smiths; and Polyphemus, at least, is child of Poseidon.) The third set are the giants Cottus, Briareus, and Gyes, each with fifty heads and a hundred hands; their Greek name, Hecatoncheires, means "hundred-handed." For their part in the battle between the gods and the Titans, see **Zeus.** The other giants, who rebelled against the gods (see **Zeus**), are in a way sons of Earth and Sky, since they sprang from the blood drops that fell to the ground when Cronus mutilated Sky (see **Cronus**).

Sky is the main consort of Earth, and it is clear that in this partnership it is the generative power of earth and the fertilizing role of the sky (by rain) that predominate, rather than any geographical concept. Earth is the principal example of a **Mother-Goddess.** In one union or another, she figures in the genealogy of all creatures except the unimportant family of **Chaos.** She mates with her son Pontus to found a remarkable race of monsters, which are described under **Sea Deities.** Finally, she produced by herself what Hesiod calls the youngest of her children, the prodigious Typhoeus, for whom see under **Zeus.**

Echidna (e-kid′na) was a monster and the mother of monsters. See **Sea Deities.**

Echo was a nymph who loved **Narcissus.**

Eileithyia (i-li-thi′ya), daughter of Zeus and **Hera,** was the goddess of childbirth.

Electra (ē-lek′tra) was (1) the daughter of Agamemnon, son of **Atreus;** (2) a daughter of Oceanus and mother by Zeus of Dardanus, founder of Troy.

Eleusis (ē-lū′sis) was the seat of the most important of the Greek mystery religions. For the myth of their founding, see **Hades** (*Persephone*).

Elysium (ē-liz′ium), or the **Elysian Fields,** was the home of the blessed in the afterlife. See **Hades** (*Underworld*).

Enceladus (en-sel′a-dus) was a giant. See **Zeus.**

Endymion (en-dim′i-on) was beloved of Selene, the moon goddess. See **Sky Deities.**

Enyalius (en-i-al′i-us), a god, and **Enyo** (ē-nī′ō), a goddess, were minor war deities and companions of Ares.

Eos (ē′os) was the dawn goddess. See **Sky Deities.**

Epaphus (ep′a-fus) was the son of Zeus and **Io.**

Epeus (e-pē′us) was the architect of the Wooden Horse in the **Trojan War** (*The fall*).

Ephialtes (ef-i-al′tēz), brother of Otus, was a giant. See **Zeus.**

The **Epigoni** (e-pig′o-nī), sons of the Seven against **Thebes,** captured the city.

Epimetheus (ep-i-mē′thūs) was the brother of Prometheus.

Erato (ĕr′a-tō) was one of the nine **Muses,** patroness of love poetry.

Erebus (ĕr′e-bus) was an area of darkness in the underworld, similar to Tartarus.

Erechtheus (e-rek′thūs) was a king of **Athens.**

Erichthonius (ĕr-ik-thōn′i-us) was (1) a king of **Athens;** (2) an early king of Troy (see **Trojan War,** *Background*).

Erigone (e-rig′ō-ne) was (1) daughter of Icarius (see **Dionysus**); (2) daughter of Aegisthus—she brought Orestes to trial and was married by Orestes in some versions of the story of the house of Atreus.

The **Erinyes** (e-rin′i-ēz) are the Furies. See **Hades** (end of article). Erinys (ĕr-in′is) is the singular form.

Eriphyle (e-rif′il-ē) was the wife of Amphiaraus of the Seven against **Thebes.**

Eris (ĕr′is) was the goddess of strife. See **Trojan War** (*Background*).

Eros (ĕr′os), who was called Amor or Cupid by the Romans, is the attendant of Aphrodite, and eventually degenerates in literature into a rotund and mischievous child, equipped with a toy bow and arrow with which he inflicts the wound of love upon mortals and deities. He was not always this figure of whimsy. In Hesiod he is a primeval power, with Earth and Tartarus, second in antiquity to Chaos alone. Later stories make him, with his brother Anteros, son of Aphrodite and Ares. The function of Anteros is somewhat dubious: he is the god of mutual love, or he avenges slighted love, or he fights against the power of Eros.

The story of Eros and Psyche ("soul") is scarcely in the range of classical mythology; it appears only late, and in a form that is intentionally allegorical. Psyche was the youngest of three daughters of a king. So beautiful was she that men forgot the worship of Aphrodite in their admiration of Psyche. Aphrodite in jealousy ordered Eros to inflict upon the girl a passion for a mean and unworthy creature. But Eros himself fell in love with her, and had her transported, in the arms of Zephyrus, to a beautiful palace, where he came to her every night. He warned her not to try to find out who he was or even what his appearance was. But Psyche's older sisters, coming to visit her, spitefully suggested that her wonderful lover was in reality a horrible monster, and for that reason kept his appearance and identity a secret. One night Psyche was overcome by curiosity, and when her lover had fallen asleep beside her she lit a candle and peeked at him. In her delighted astonishment at seeing the comely Eros, she spilled a drop of candle wax on his arm; he awoke and fled, and did not return. Psyche wandered everywhere in search of him, and at last came to the palace of Aphrodite, for whom she had to perform three apparently impossible tasks in order to gain the goddess's forgiveness and to be reunited with Eros. The first task was to sort out a great pile of various grains into their proper heaps; a horde of ants, sent by Eros, achieved this for her. Then she was required to collect a tuft of wool from each member of a huge flock; a river god kindly told her that she could manage this by waiting until the sheep went to their watering place, and then picking tufts of wool off the briars that grew by the stream. Finally she was sent to the underworld to get a precious box of ointments from Persephone. Persephone gave her the box, and warned her not to open it. But Psyche again could not control her curiosity. She opened the box, and was about to be swept back to the underworld forever, when Eros intervened and prevailed on Zeus to grant immortality to Psyche, and on Aphrodite to be reconciled to her. Thus Eros and Psyche were reunited and dwelt together in heaven.

The most famous record of the story of Eros and Psyche is in the Latin prose romance of Apuleius (second century A.D.) called the *Metamorphoses*. Robert Bridges has a narrative poem, *Eros and Psyche* (1885). See also Keats's *Ode to Psyche* (1820).

Erymanthus (ĕr-i-man'thus) is a mountain in Arcadia, and home of the boar caught by **Heracles** (third Labor).

Erysichthon (ĕr-i-sik'thon) was punished by **Demeter.**

Eryx (ĕr'ix) is (1) a mountain in west Sicily, associated with the worship of Venus; (2) a son of Poseidon with whom **Heracles** wrestled (tenth Labor).

Eteocles (e-tē'ō-klēz) was one of Oedipus' sons and a figure in the story of the Seven against **Thebes.**

Eumaeus (ū-mē'us) was the faithful swineherd of **Odysseus** (*Ithaca*).

The **Eumenides** (ū-men'i-dēz) are "the kindly ones," a euphemism for the Furies. See **Hades** (end of article).

Euphrosyne (ū-fros'i-nē) was one of the three **Charites** (Graces).

Europa (ū-rō'pa) was carried by Zeus, in bull form, to **Crete.**

Eurus (ū'rus) is the east wind. See **Wind Deities.**

Euryalus (ū-rī'a-lus) took part in a night raid with Nisus. See **Aeneas** (*Italy*).

Eurydice (ū-rid'i-sē) was (1) the wife of **Orpheus;** (2) the wife of Creon of **Thebes** (*Antigone*).

Eurypylus (ū-rip'i-lus), son of Telephus, fought for Troy and was killed by Neoptolemus in the **Trojan War** (*Late events*).

Eurystheus (ū-ris'thūs) was the taskmaster of Heracles.

Eurytion (ū-rit'i-on) was (1) a hunter killed by Peleus in the **Calydonian Boar Hunt;** (2) the herdsman of Geryon (see **Heracles,** tenth Labor); (3) a centaur killed by **Heracles** (sixth Labor).

Euterpe (ū-tur'pē) was one of the nine **Muses,** patroness of lyric poetry and the flute.

Evander (ē-van'der) was from Arcadia, and ruled a city on the site of Rome. He was an ally of **Aeneas** (*Italy*).

The **Fates,** called Moirae by the Greeks, Parcae by the Romans, were thought of as the dispensers of each person's lot in life, assigned at birth. The Fates are represented as three old women, and their allotting of fate as a process of spinning, measuring, and cutting a thread. Clotho spins the thread, Lachesis determines its length, and Atropos cuts it off when the time comes. In Roman thought fate is often the impersonally conceived Fatum. In Greek, *Tyche* (Luck or Fortune) and *Ananke* (Necessity) are concepts closely related to fate.

Faunus (faw'nus) was often identified with **Pan.** The fauns were woodland creatures like satyrs.

Favonius (fa-vō'ni-us) is the Roman name for Zephyrus, the west wind. See **Wind Deities.**

Flora (flor'a) was the Roman goddess of flowers, resembling the Greek **Chloris.**

The **Furies** were the spirits who punished crimes, especially crimes committed within the family circle. See **Hades** (end of article).

Gaea (jē'a), **Gaia** (jā'a), or **Ge** (jē) is Mother Earth. See **Earth and Sky.**

Galatea (gal-a-tē'a) was (1) a Nereid loved by Polyphemus (see **Sea Deities**); (2) in some modern versions, the wife of **Pygmalion.**

Ganymede (gan'i-mēd), or **Ganymedes** (gan-i-mē'dēz), was a Trojan prince who became Zeus's cupbearer. See **Trojan War** (*Background*).

Gemini (jem'i-ni), the "Twins," were the Dioscuri, Castor and Polydeuces, sons of **Leda.**

Geryon (jĕr'i-on) was a three-bodied man whose cattle were taken by **Heracles** (tenth Labor).

The **Giants** are famous chiefly for their war against **Zeus.**

Glauce (glaw'sē) was a Corinthian princess, bride of Jason. See **Argonauts.**

Glaucus (glaw'cus) was (1) a fisherman who became a **Sea Deity;** (2) an ally of the Trojans in the Trojan War.

The **Golden Age** was the first of the **Ages of Man.**

The **Gorgons** (gor'gonz) were three hideous sisters, one of whom, Medusa, was killed by **Perseus.** See also **Sea Deities.**

The **Graces,** also called the **Charites,** were daughters of Zeus.

The **Graeae** (grē'ē), or **Graiae** (grā'ē), the "Gray Ones," were the sisters and guardians of the Gorgons. See **Perseus** and **Sea Deities.**

Gyes (jī'ēz) was one of the three hundred-handed giants, sons of **Earth and Sky.**

Hades (hā'dēz), the king of the underworld, is son of **Cronus** and Rhea. He is like his brother Zeus in appearance, mature, dignified, bearded, but somewhat grimmer. Two things that Hades is *not* should be noted: he is not a devil and he is not, as a general rule, a place. The use of Hades to mean the underworld, though common parlance today, is not common in ancient myth, and poets of all periods are more likely than not to keep the ancient usage. Hades means the Unseen One. There is no dominant Roman name for him. In both Greek and Latin he is called also Pluto, which probably is in origin the same as Plutus, the god of wealth; it makes sense, in an agrarian society, for the god of wealth to be underground, since wealth comes from the ground. The Romans sometimes called him Dis, which also means the god of wealth, and Orcus, from Greek *horkos*, "oath," presumably the name of a god of oaths.

Persephone. The wife of Hades is Persephone, Proserpina in Latin, often called simply Cora, "the maiden." She is daughter of Demeter, the goddess of grain, and the story of her abduction by Hades and of the sequel to it is one of the most familiar of myths. While gathering posies one day in the vale of Enna, in Sicily, the maiden Persephone, tugging at one large and beautiful flower, found that as she pulled it a great hole opened in the ground. From it Hades came forth and carried her off to his dark kingdom. Demeter searched distractedly for her daughter; while she grieved, no crops grew and famine threatened the world. In her wanderings she came to Eleusis, in Attica, where, disguised as a poor old woman, she was taken home by the daughters of King Celeus of Eleusis and became nursemaid of the king's infant son Demophoon. Demeter would have made her young charge immortal, and to that end laid him nightly in the fire, to burn away his mortality. But this divine plan was interrupted by the child's mother, Metanira, who, seeing the performance by chance, screamed so piercingly that Demeter, startled, cast the baby aside and assumed her own form. Rebuking Metanira, she ordered a temple to be built, and imparted to the

Eleusinians certain secret rites which were to become an annual celebration in her honor.

At length Demeter learned that Hades had taken her daughter. Zeus then sent Hermes to bid Hades restore the girl to her mother so that the whole world would not starve. Hades consented, but made sure beforehand that Persephone had eaten some pomegranate seeds while in his kingdom. This fact meant that she could never leave the underworld permanently. A compromise was arranged: Persephone was to spend one third of the year with her husband, Hades, below ground, and two thirds with her mother, Demeter, on earth.

The main symbolism of the story is plain enough: Persephone represents the annual cycle of vegetation, and at the end of the story it is often said that the third of the year that she spends underground is the period in which the fields are bare. Some of the details of Demeter's visit to Eleusis are less apparent in meaning; they have to do with the Eleusinian Mysteries, the religious celebrations of a large cult whose beliefs and rites were secret but certainly were connected with the annual "death" and "rebirth" of the crops, and perhaps included the idea of the rebirth or survival of man after death.

Underworld. The description of the realm of Hades varies in different myths and different ages. Usually it is underground, entered by caves such as Taenarum near Sparta, but sometimes, as in the story of Odysseus, it seems to be in the far west.

The chief geographical features are the five rivers, Styx, Acheron, Pyriphlegethon, Cocytus, and Lethe. It is a gloomy, dark, and barren region, its only vegetation the weed asphodel. The souls of the dead are unhappy and almost spiritless shades. Achilles tells Odysseus in the *Odyssey* that it is better to be a serf to a poor man on earth than to be ruler of all the dead. But sometimes, particularly in later descriptions, notably in the *Aeneid,* 6 (where, however, there is much that is philosophy rather than myth), there are distinct divisions of the underworld. Some few fortunate souls (such as Menelaus and Diomedes) are transported, still living, to Elysium, a place of happiness like the Isles of the Blest, whither Achilles is sometimes said to go. The place of punishment is Tartarus, which is generally located deep down in terrible gloom. Hither the Titans and the Giants were hurled by Zeus, and here Prometheus was imprisoned during part of his enchainment. Here too are located the outstanding human sinners of myth. Tantalus, who served his own son Pelops to the gods at a banquet, to test their omniscience, stands here in a pool of water, with boughs of fruit trees overhead; he is eternally tantalized, for when he stoops to drink, the water recedes, and when he reaches for fruit, the boughs sway out of reach. The cunning Sisyphus cheated death for a while by bidding his wife Merope leave him unburied and then gaining Hades' permission to return to earth to punish his wife for the heinous offense of not burying him; when old age brought him again below ground he went to Tartarus, where he rolls a huge rock up a cliff, only to have it roll down again as he reaches the top. The giant Tityus, who attempted to rape Leto, mother of Apollo and Artemis, lies tied to the ground while vultures eat constantly at his liver. Ixion tried to seduce Hera but was foiled, and turns forever on a wheel in Tartarus. The Danaids, who slew their bridegrooms on their wedding night, are in Tartarus pouring water into leaky jars.

There are numerous attendants of the infernal monarch. The three judges, who assign the dead to their places, are Minos, king of Crete, Rhadamanthus, also of Crete, and Aeacus of Aegina. Charon is the ferryman who conveys the dead across the river (Styx or Acheron) that bounds the underworld; he is surly, old, and unkempt, and demands as ferrying fee an obol (a penny). The Greeks often buried their dead with an obol in their mouths to pay Charon. Cerberus, the three-headed (sometimes two heads, sometimes fifty) dog, stands guard before the house of Hades, fawning on those who enter; but those who seek to leave he devours. Also associated with the nether regions are the three Furies (Erinyes), Alecto, Megaera, and Tisiphone, who sprang from the blood drops when **Cronus** mutilated his father. They are avengers of crimes, especially of murder and crimes committed against a parent or other close blood relative. They are just but pitiless, terrible to behold, pursuing their victims with snakes, torches, or whips. Their best-known victims are Orestes (see **Atreus**) and Alcmaeon (see **Thebes,** *Epigoni*).

The story of the rape of Persephone is told in the *Homeric Hymn to Demeter*. See also Swinburne, *The Garden of Proserpine* (1866), Meredith, *The Day of the Daughter of Hades* (1883), Tennyson, *Demeter and Persephone* (1889), and Browning, *Ixion* (1883).

Haemon (hē′mon) was the son of Creon of **Thebes,** and the lover of Antigone.

Hamadryads (ham-a-drī′adz) were tree **nymphs.**

Harmonia (har-mō′ni-a) was the wife of Cadmus, founder of **Thebes.**

Harpies (har′pēz) were monstrous bird-women who tormented Phineus (see **Argonauts,** *Outward voyage*) and were encountered by **Aeneas** (*Wanderings*). See also **Sea Deities.**

Hebe (hē′bē), daughter of Zeus and Hera, was goddess of youth, cupbearer of the gods, and bride of Heracles.

Hecate (hek′a-tē), daughter of Asteria and Perses (both children of Titans), was a goddess of three provinces or functions, and is consequently often referred to as "triple Hecate" and depicted in art as having three bodies. She was a moon goddess, a goddess of the crossroads on earth, and a goddess of the underworld. Her usual weapon or badge is a torch or torches. As a moon goddess she is often identified with Artemis. In connection with her control of the crossroads and with her underworld nature, Hecate was the queen of black magic and the patroness of witches.

Hector (hek′tor), son of Priam, was the great defender of Troy in the **Trojan War.**

Hecuba (hek′ū-ba), or **Hecabe** (hek′a-bē), was the wife of King Priam of Troy. See **Trojan War.**

Helen, daughter of Zeus and **Leda,** was the immediate cause of the **Trojan War** (*Rallying of the host*).

Helenus (hel′e-nus) was a prophet and a son of Priam. He is a figure in the **Trojan War** (*Late events*).

Helicon (hel′i-kon), a mountain in Boeotia, was sacred to the Muses.

Helius (hē′li-us) was the sun god. See **Sky Deities.**

Helle (hel′ē) was rescued by the ram of the golden fleece, but later drowned. See **Argonauts** (*Background*).

Hellen (hel′en), son of **Deucalion,** was the eponym of the Greeks (Hellenes).

Hephaestus (he-fes′tus), Roman Vulcan or Mulciber, son of Hera without father (but in Homer son of Zeus and Hera), is god of fire and the forge. He is mature, bearded, usually dressed as a workman, and shown wearing an artisan's skullcap and carrying hammer and tongs. Sometimes he is shown at the forge with his assistants, the Cyclopes. He is often associated with vol canic (from Vulcan) islands, such as Lemnos in the Aegean and the Lipari Islands north of Sicily. He is lame, and was born so. Hera, ashamed of her defective child, threw him down from heaven or Olympus. He landed in the sea and was tended by the Nereids Thetis and Eurynome. For nine years he stayed on earth, and before returning he made a splendid throne and sent it as a gift for his mother. When Hera sat in it she found herself caught in an invisible and unbreakable net, from which only Hephaestus could extricate her. He refused to come home and do so, until Dionysus got him drunk and persuaded him to relent. Later, Hephaestus was again hurled from the divine home, this time by Zeus when Hephaestus tried to make peace during a quarrel between Zeus and Hera. He fell all day, "And with the setting sun Dropt from the zenith, like a falling star, On Lemnos" (Milton, *Paradise Lost,* 1.744–746).

His role in myth is chiefly that of craftsman. The most famous of his many forgings was the set of armor which he made for Achilles during the Trojan War; it, especially the shield, is described in the *Iliad.* He is in Homer a figure of fun; the gods laugh at him as he serves as cupbearer. In the *Iliad* he is not prominent in the battles, but on one occasion he fights against the river Xanthus and defeats him by drying up his stream.

He is usually said to have as wife Aphrodite. For the story of one of her infidelities with Ares and how Hephaestus got revenge, see under **Aphrodite.** In the *Iliad* he is married to Charis (Grace).

Hephaestus is the maker of all sorts of wonderful things that are mentioned in myths, such as the brazen bulls and the brazen man, Talos, which come into the story of the **Argonauts,** the necklace of Harmonia of **Thebes,** the ball of thread used by **Theseus** in the Labyrinth, and the rattle used by **Heracles** against the Stymphalian birds.

Hera (hē′ra), the Roman Juno, is daughter of Cronus and Rhea and wife of her brother Zeus. She is a frequent, rather than a prominent, figure in myth, with little personality apart from her relation to Zeus. As queen of the Olympians she is represented as a handsome, mature woman, often crowned, bearing a scepter, accompanied by her sacred bird, the peacock, whose tail is adorned with the hundred eyes of Argus, the guard of **Io.** She is more interesting as wife than as queen. Her willfulness in this role and her tendency to nag her husband are conspicuous from Homer on down. Most familiar of all is her role as the jealous wife, spying on Zeus's love affairs, persecuting his mistresses (see **Io** and Semele, mother of **Dionysus**), and vindictive toward the heroic offspring of these liaisons, especially toward **Heracles** (*Birth*). But she can on occasion be the sponsor of heroes, as Athena often is; Jason of the **Argonauts** is the best-known favorite of Hera.

Hera is a wife goddess rather than a mother-goddess. She is especially associated with the marriage rite (as in the story of **Aeneas** and Dido in the *Aeneid,* 4). She is a goddess of women, sometimes of childbirth, especially as Roman Juno. Then she is called Juno Lucina, incorporating into herself the birth goddess Lucina, whose Greek counterpart is **Eileithyia.**

With Zeus as father, she had three or four children: **Hebe,** goddess of youth, **Ares,** god of war, Eileithyia, and **Hephaestus,** the divine craftsman and god of the forge; in Homer Hephaestus seems to be son of Zeus and Hera, but Hesiod says that Hera produced him apart from Zeus (apparently with no father) in retaliation for Zeus's production of **Athena** from his forehead. One other child is sometimes ascribed to Hera, the monster Typhaon (Typhoeus, Typhon), who waged war against **Zeus;** he, too, was apparently fatherless.

Heracles (hĕr′a-klēz), called Hercules by the Romans, is the greatest of all mythological slayers of giants and monsters; he is the roving, never-resting toiler, and the performer of seemingly impossible tasks. Though there is reason to believe that in early stories he may have been of normal or even small stature, he is most familiar as a muscular giant, clad in a lion skin, bearing a mighty club and a bow and quiver. His strength is usually employed for morally good purposes, and his slaying of monsters is often represented as a purification of the world from evil powers. Yet poets have not infrequently, on the other hand, made him a mere muscle man, devoid of judgment and intellect.

Background. He is the son of Zeus. But his human background is also of mythological importance. One son of the hero Perseus was Electryon, king of Mycenae; another was Alcaeus. All Electryon's sons having been killed in battle with the Teleboans, Alcaeus' son, Amphitryon, was made ruler over Mycenae when Electryon went on an expedition to gain revenge on the Teleboans. Amphitryon married Electryon's daughter, Alcmena. When Electryon returned, Amphitryon accidentally killed him, and had to go into exile as a result. Sthenelus, another descendant of Perseus, became king of Mycenae. Amphitryon went to Thebes, and there was able to help Creon, the king, whose fields were being devastated by a tremendous, uncatchable fox. Amphitryon was able to borrow from Cephalus of Athens an inescapable hound. The dilemma of the consequent hunt was solved by Zeus, who turned both fox and hound to stone.

Next Amphitryon, still seeking revenge for the death of Electryon's sons, made an attack on the Teleboans. He succeeded, as follows. Their king, Pterelaus, had a golden hair on his head, and as long as it remained there he was invincible. He had also a daughter, Comaetho, who fell in love with Amphitryon, and for his sake pulled out her father's golden hair, thus causing his death and her countrymen's defeat. As a reward for her treachery Amphitryon had her put to death. (For a very similar story, see Nisus, Scylla, and Minos, under **Athens.**)

Birth. On the very night on which Amphitryon was to return from the expedition, Zeus, who had fallen in love with Alcmena, came to her disguised as Amphitryon. In honor of the occasion Zeus made the night last three times its normal length. Before morning, Zeus left and the real Amphitryon arrived. Numerous playwrights, from Plautus until now, have exploited the comic possibilities of the confusion of persons. The result of the night's activities was that Alcmena conceived twins, Heracles by Zeus and Iphicles by Amphitryon. The day that Heracles was due to be born, Hera, jealous of Alcmena and hostile to Heracles, prevailed upon the goddess of birth, Eileithyia, to delay his birth and speed up the birth of another descendant of Perseus, because it was destined (or announced by Zeus) that the descendant of Perseus born on that day would be ruler of all about him. And so Eurystheus, son of Sthenelus, was born that day and became king of Mycenae, while Heracles, born soon after, had to serve him. Eventually, though not in time to foil Hera's jealous plot, a maidservant of Alcmena, Galanthis, tricked Eileithyia into breaking the spell by which she was delaying Heracles' birth. Alcmena was released from her pains, and Galanthis was turned by the vindictive Hera into a weasel. No sooner was Heracles born (though some writers put this story several months later) than two great snakes, sent, of course, by Hera, attacked his cradle by night. While Iphicles shrank away and cried for help, Heracles strangled the snakes with his bare hands, thus clearly revealing his divine parentage. He is, however, sometimes called Alcides, after his nominal grandfather, Amphitryon's father, Alcaeus.

After a childhood in which he was trained in various arts and skills by the very best teachers (Polydeuces taught him boxing, Linus, a son of Apollo, music; Heracles is sometimes said to have killed Linus with a blow of the lyre because Linus cuffed him), Heracles spent his entire life in the performance of prodigious deeds. It is not feasible to give an inclusive account of them, but certain deeds and incidents are outstanding, above all the famous Twelve Labors of Heracles, which he is usually supposed to have performed at the bidding of his taskmaster, King Eurystheus. The twelve are not the same in all stories, but those given here are close to being canonical. In addition to the Twelve Labors, there are numerous *parerga,* or side tasks, which can conveniently be included with the Labors, and an endless number of Deeds, some of which will be mentioned later.

Labors. The order as well as the roster of the Labors varies, but in first place always comes the killing of the Nemean lion, a fierce beast with a hide impervious to cutting weapons. Heracles subdued the lion with his club and then strangled it and flayed it, using its own claws to penetrate the hide. The lion's skin was thenceforth the armor of Heracles. The Hydra of the swamp of Lerna was a formidable monster with numerous heads (nine, or one hundred), one of them immortal. In this second Labor Heracles was assisted by his nephew and frequent companion, Iolaus, son of Iphicles. On attacking the creature, Heracles found that as soon as he cut off or clubbed one head, two more would grow on the spot; and so Iolaus burned the "roots" where each had grown, and this prevented new heads from growing. The immortal head Heracles buried under a rock. To even the fight, Hera sent a giant crab to help the Hydra. The crab bit Heracles in the foot, and for its services was made a constellation by Hera. Heracles dipped his arrows in the gore of the Hydra, thus making them venomous.

Third comes the Erymanthian boar, which Heracles was required to bring back alive to Eurystheus. After chasing it into deep snow, on Mount Erymanthus in Arcadia, Heracles caught it, brought it to Eurystheus, and flung it at the terrified king, who had taken refuge in a large jar. While pursuing the boar, Heracles fell in with the centaur Pholus, who entertained him. Other centaurs also came, and somehow a fight broke out, in the course of which Chiron, the wise and immortal centaur, was wounded by one of Heracles' poisoned arrows. In agony, he wished for death but could not have it until Prometheus took on his immortality for him and Chiron died. The fourth Labor is another chase. Heracles had to bring alive to Mycenae the Cerynean hind, a wondrous animal with golden antlers and brazen hoofs. After a year's pursuit, Heracles caught the hind. Fifthly, Heracles had the task of removing from a lake near the town of Stymphalus in Arcadia certain birds which are called the Stymphalian birds. They are sometimes said to be man-eaters, sometimes to be a menace simply by dint of their numbers. With the aid of a brazen rattle (supplied by Athena, made by Hephaestus) Heracles frightened the birds away. The sixth Labor was the cleansing of the Augean Stables. Augeas, king of Elis, had three thousand cattle; their stalls had not been cleaned for thirty years. By diverting the course of the rivers Alpheus and Peneus through the stables, Heracles finished the job in one day. He was to have been paid for this task, but Augeas withheld the pay when he learned that the task had been assigned by Eurystheus. Heracles later returned and killed Augeas in revenge; he killed also Augeas' allies, the Molionids, Siamese twin giants, sons of Poseidon and Molione. A side adventure on this occasion was the killing of the centaur Eurytion, to prevent the centaur from taking as wife Mnesimache, daughter of Dexamenus, at whose house Heracles was being entertained.

All six of the Labors hitherto mentioned take place in the northern part of the Peloponnesus, and concern creatures barely, if at all, familiar in other stories. In the remaining six, the geographical range is much broader, and most of the exploits touch on things and places eminent in mythology apart from Heracles. The seventh Labor concerns the Cretan Bull, which Heracles captured and brought from Crete to Mycenae. It later escaped and made its way to Marathon, where it provided an exploit for Theseus. This is said to have been the bull that fathered the Minotaur, for which see under **Theseus.** Eighth was the capture of the man-eating mares of Diomedes, king of the Bistonians, in Thrace. Either Heracles fed Diomedes to his mares, upon which they became gentle, or Heracles, at the head of an army, overcame the Bistonians, killed Diomedes, and entrusted the mares to a certain Abderus. Abderus was dragged to death by the mares, and in his memory Heracles founded the city of Abdera near his grave. Ninth is the capture of the girdle or belt of Hippolyte, queen of the Amazons. Heracles sailed with a crew of warriors to fetch this object for Admete, daughter of Eurystheus. Hippolyte was willing to give it as a gift when Heracles asked for it, but Hera stirred up a fight and in it Heracles killed Hippolyte and took the girdle. Of the numerous *parerga* attending this expedition only one need be mentioned. When Heracles put in at Troy, he found that the city was suffering from both a pestilence sent by Apollo, and a sea monster sent by Poseidon. These visitations were the revenge of the two gods, who had built a wall around the city and then had been cheated by King Laomedon of the pay for which they had contracted. Oracular information revealed that the city would be saved from its two calamities only if Laomedon's beautiful daughter, Hesione, were sacrificed to the sea monster. When Heracles arrived, the girl was chained to the rocks, awaiting her fate. Heracles offered to save her but stipulated that he be given a prize—not the girl, but certain famous mares belonging to Laomedon. Heracles killed the monster, but again Laomedon refused to pay. Heracles departed but returned later with a fleet, took the city, and killed Laomedon. This time Hesione was taken as booty and given to Heracles' ally Telamon; their son was Teucer of the Trojan War.

Next (tenth) Heracles went to an island in the far west to bring back the oxen of the three-bodied man, Geryon. It was a long and toilsome journey to reach Geryon's island. Heracles sailed the stream of Oceanus in the golden cup of Helius, the sun, and passing between Europe and Africa raised two mountains to form the Pillars of Heracles, between which lie the Straits of Gibraltar. The oxen were guarded by a giant herdsman, Eurytion, and a two- or three-headed dog, Orth(r)us. Heracles killed them both and also their master Geryon. Driving the cattle back to Mycenae was an arduous task, and Heracles had to protect his flock from various perils, including rustlers, two of whom are worthy of mention. In Sicily, Eryx, son of Poseidon, stole a bull, and to regain it Heracles had to defeat him in a wrestling match. On the site of Rome, a giant named Cacus stole several oxen and dragged them backward (to disguise their trail, as **Hermes** did in stealing Apollo's cattle) into a cave. Heracles discovered the trick when some of the cattle in the cave answered the lowing of the others. The cattle were recovered and Cacus was killed.

There were originally to have been only ten Labors, but Eurystheus refused to count two of those done: the Lernaean Hydra, because Iolaus had helped, and the cleansing of the Augean Stables, because it had been done for hire (though the pay was withheld); and so two more tasks were added. The eleventh was to bring to Mycenae the golden apples of the Garden of the Hesperides (the "daughters of evening") in the far west. The apples grew on a tree, tended by the Hesperides and guarded by a serpent, Ladon. Heracles killed Ladon, and, in some versions, persuaded the giant Atlas, who also lived nearby, to fetch the apples for him. He offered to take over meanwhile Atlas's burden of sustaining heaven on his shoulders. Delighted to shed his load, Atlas fetched the apples and then proposed to take them to Mycenae himself, leaving Heracles permanently with heaven on his shoulders. Heracles feigned acquiescence but asked Atlas to take back the burden just for a moment while he got a cushion for his shoulders to make the task more comfortable. Thus he tricked the giant (giants in myths are usually stupid) into resuming his task forever.

The twelfth and final Labor was to bring Cerberus, the three-headed dog of the underworld, to Eurystheus. Gaining entrance to the underworld through a cave, and winning Hades' permission to take Cerberus provided he did not kill him, Heracles, aided by Hermes and Athena, managed to chain the beast, take him up and show him to Eurystheus, and then return him to the underworld. It is sometimes said that on this same trip he rescued **Theseus** (*Later adventures*) from the underworld.

Minor stories. Of the other feats of Heracles, only a few can be listed. One of the earliest was the killing on Mount Cithaeron of a lion, the hide of which is sometimes said to be his garment, instead of the hide of the Nemean Lion. Among the giants whom he dispatched were Antaeus, son of

Earth, whose strength was ever renewed so long as he touched the ground—Heracles held Antaeus aloft and strangled him; Cycnus, a robber and a giant, son of Ares; Lycaon, brother of Cycnus; and Alcyoneus, whom Heracles killed during the battle of the gods and the Giants (see under **Zeus**). Busiris, king of Egypt, made a practice of sacrificing to Zeus all strangers who visited his realm. Heracles overcame the king's entire police force and then put Busiris himself to death. Also in Africa, Heracles had an encounter with the Pygmies, who attacked him while he slept, and with a curious folk called the Cercopes, small apelike men. Heracles caught and carried off samples of both species.

Heracles was not happy in his domestic life. His first wife was the Theban princess, Megara, given him in marriage for his service in freeing Thebes from the rule of neighboring Orchomenus. Heracles, having met envoys from Orchomenus on their way to collect tribute, cut off their ears and noses and told them tó carry *that* tribute back home; the Orchomenians at once attacked Thebes and were defeated, chiefly by Heracles. After several years of marriage with Megara, Heracles was driven mad by Hera and killed his own children. In some versions Megara, too, is killed; in others she survives and is later given by Heracles in marriage to Iolaus. For this involuntary killing Heracles required purification, and when he sought it at Delphi he was told to serve Eurystheus for twelve years.

On a later occasion, too, Heracles sought purification at Delphi, after he had killed a friend, Iphitus, either in a second fit of madness or when drunk. He had gone first to King Neleus of Pylos to be purified, and had been refused. At Delphi he was purified, but still suffered from a disease, and was ordered by his brother Apollo to serve as a slave under Queen Omphale of Lydia for one year. Before leaving the shrine, Heracles attempted to make off with the sacred tripod; Apollo also seized it, and Zeus had to part his quarreling sons with a thunderbolt. For a year, then, Heracles performed all kinds of female tasks as the slave of Omphale. After release from bondage he took vengeance on Neleus for refusing to purify him. He attacked Pylos, killed Neleus and all his twelve sons except Nestor (of the Trojan War), including Periclymenus, who had the power of changing shape while in battle, and even wounded Hades, who joined the battle for the men of Pylos. At about this time Heracles seduced the Arcadian princess, Auge. She exposed the child who was consequently born. Suckled by a doe, the child survived and grew up to be Telephus, who became king of Teuthrania, in Asia Minor, and is a minor figure in the story of the Trojan War.

Many more stories concern Heracles in minor roles, but these are told elsewhere: he is in the story of **Alcestis,** he sometimes is one of the **Argonauts** (*Outward voyage*), he rescues **Prometheus.**

Deianira. At some point in his career, Heracles took as his bride Deianira, daughter of King Oeneus of Calydon. He had to overcome another suitor, the river god Achelous, who assumed the form of a dragon and a bull during their wrestling match. Early in their marriage, while they were crossing a river, Heracles entrusted Deianira to the centaur Nessus, who acted as a sort of ferry across the river. Nessus attempted to rape Deianira after carrying her across the river, and was promptly shot and killed by one of Heracles' venomous arrows. As he died, Nessus persuaded Deianira to take some of his blood, poisoned by the arrow, and keep it hidden away to use as a philter if ever she should need such assistance to keep Heracles' love. Later on, Heracles fell in love with Iole, daughter of King Eurytus of Oechalia, and sacked Oechalia to get her. He brought Iole home as a concubine. Deianira learned of her husband's love for the girl and decided to try the philter. She smeared it on a robe and sent the robe to Heracles as a welcoming gift. When Heracles put it on and came near an altar fire (he was sacrificing to Zeus), it at once consumed his flesh. This was the end of Heracles. He bade his son Hyllus (by Deianira) place him still living on a funeral pyre on Mount Oeta. Then Poeas, father of Philoctetes of the Trojan War, lighted the pyre, and as a reward was given the bow and arrows of Heracles. Heracles rose to heaven, the mortal part of him being burned away, and was there reconciled with Hera and married to her daughter, Hebe, the goddess of youth. Deianira took her own life.

There are a number of follow-up stories to the legend of Heracles, involving his sons and descendants, the Heraclidae. The most important of these stories concerns the pursuit by Eurystheus of Hyllus and the other sons of Heracles into Attica, and the defeat and death of Eurystheus. Macaria, daughter of Heracles and Deianira, took her own life when an oracle foretold that the Heraclidae would be victorious if a child of Heracles died voluntarily. Later on, Cresphontes, a great-grandson of Heracles and king of Messene, was murdered by his cousin, Polyphontes, and his widow Merope was forced to marry Polyphontes. But Aegyptus, son of Merope and Cresphontes, when he grew to maturity killed Polyphontes and thus recovered his father's kingdom. Eventually the descendants of Heracles became kings of Sparta.

In volume of literary treatment, if not in deference accorded, Amphitryon has far outstripped his illustrious foster son, and is one of the best-loved subjects for comic drama. The contemporary French playwright Jean Giraudoux called his play about him *Amphitryon 38*, because, according to his (conservative) count, his was the thirty-eighth version. Among his predecessors were Plautus, Dryden, and Molière. See Lindberger, *The Transformations of Amphitryon* (1956). Euripides (*Heracles*), Sophocles (*Trachinian Women*), and Seneca (*Hercules Furens* and *Hercules Oetaeus*) all wrote plays about the great toiler. Merope, too, has been the subject of plays: Voltaire (1743), Alfieri (1783), and Matthew Arnold (1858).

Hercules (hur′kū-lēz) is **Heracles.**

Hermaphroditus (hur-ma-frō-di′tus) was the son of **Hermes** and Aphrodite.

Hermes (hur′mēz), Roman Mercury, son of Zeus and Maia, daughter of Atlas, is the herald and messenger of the gods. He is pictured as a youth, usually beardless and slender of build, equipped with messenger's wand (the caduceus, which in its most elaborate form has two snakes twined about it) and traveler's hat (the petasus, a low-crowned, broad-brimmed cap); he often has wings at his ankles, on his shoulders, and on his hat.

Though in myth Hermes is most familiar as a messenger, he has many interests and powers. He is the god of lucky finds, the patron of eloquence, and of thieves and rogues, a god of flocks and shepherds, and the guide of travelers, especially of souls on the way to the underworld, in which role he is known as Hermes Psychopompus. He is called Argiphontes (Slayer of Argus) from his part in the story of **Io**.

A number of his powers are implicit in the most famous story about him, the story of his birth and first day of life. This delightful account of divine roguery is found in the *Homeric Hymn to Hermes*, among English translations of which is Shelley's. Hermes was born of Maía in a cave on Mount Cyllene in Arcadia. By noon he had invented the lyre (made from a turtle shell), by evening he had stolen a herd of cattle from his half-brother Apollo, and by next morning he was back in his cradle, sleeping as sweetly as any other baby. The story is full of evidence of Hermes' deceitful eloquence and of his cunning; in stealing the cattle, for example, he made them walk backward to confuse the trail for a pursuer. A detail of this story not in the *Hymn* but mentioned by Ovid is that Hermes, while stealing the cattle, met an old man named Battus. He bribed Battus with a heifer not to tell anybody that he had seen the cattle, and a little later, to test Battus, went back to him in disguise and asked if he had seen any cattle, offering a larger bribe for information. Battus promptly told, and Hermes forthwith turned him into a touchstone.

Hermes once fell in love with Herse, one of the three daughters of Cecrops, king of Athens. When he went to call on her he encountered her sister Aglaurus. Athena, still angry over the incident of Erichthonius (see **Athena,** where a conflicting story about these sisters is told), caused Aglaurus to be consumed by envy of her sister for her good fortune in having so handsome a lover. Aglaurus therefore attempted to bar Hermes' way, and was for this turned into a black stone. This proclivity to turn his enemies into stone probably has some connection with the "stony" aspect of Hermes' own nature: heaps of stones were often piled in his honor at crossroads and other points by travelers, and the square stone pillars called herms are no doubt related to this old practice.

Hermes had three sons of mythological interest, Pan, Hermaphroditus, and Autolycus. **Pan** requires a separate article. Hermaphroditus, son of Hermes and Aphrodite, was a handsome youth. The water nymph Salmacis fell in love with him, but the youth was unresponsive. One day, unwittingly, he took a swim in her own spring; Salmacis embraced him and prayed that they might never be parted. And so it turned out: they were fused into a single body, a hermaphrodite. Autolycus, famous as a thief, a liar, and a wrestler, was Heracles' wrestling teacher.

Hermione (hur-mǐ′ō-nē) was the daughter of Helen and Menelaus. See **Atreus** (end of article).

Hero (hē′rō) and **Leander.** Leander of Abydus loved Hero, priestess of Aphrodite at Sestus, a town just across the Hellespont from Abydus. Every night Leander would swim the Hellespont to visit Hero, until one stormy night he was drowned in the attempt. His body was washed up at Sestus next day, and was discovered by Hero, who then plunged to death in the waves. The theme is treated by Ovid in the *Heroides,* by the Greek poet Musaeus (sixth century A.D.), and in *Hero and Leander,* begun by Christopher Marlowe and finished by George Chapman. Byron mentions the story briefly in the *Bride of Abydos*, 2, referring to

> ". . . that night of stormy water
> When Love, who sent, forgot to save
> The young, the beautiful, the brave."

Herse (hur′sē) was a daughter of Cecrops, king of Athens. See **Athena** and **Hermes.**

Hesione (hē-sī′ō-nē), daughter of Laomedon, king of Troy, was given to Telamon by **Heracles** (ninth Labor).

Hesperia (hes-pěr′i-a), "the land of the evening," is a name for Italy.

* The **Hesperides** (hes-pěr′i-dēz) dwelt in a garden in the far west in which there were apples of gold. See **Heracles** (eleventh Labor).

Hesperus (hes′per-us) is the evening star.

Hestia (hes′ti-a), Roman Vesta, is the eldest child of Cronus and Rhea. Like her sister Demeter, she is a mature and dignified figure. She is a virgin. In her Roman form Vesta has, as her priestesses, six Vestal Virgins, and her worship in Rome goes back to very early times. She represents the home and especially the hearth. She is not an important figure in myth.

Hippocrene (hip-o-krē′nē) was a spring on Mount Helicon, and was sacred to the **Muses.**

Hippodamia (hip-o-da-mē′a) was (1) the bride of Pirithous, friend of **Theseus** (*Later adventures*); (2) the bride of **Pelops.**

Hippolyte (hi-pol′i-tē), or **Hippolyta,** was (1) the queen of the **Amazons,** who was killed by **Heracles** (ninth Labor); the Amazon abducted by **Theseus** (*Later adventures*) is sometimes given this name; (2) wife of Acastus (see **Salmoneus**).

*read: (hes-pěr′ i-dēz), daughters of Hesperus,

Hippolytus (hi-pol′i-tus), the son of **Theseus,** was beloved of Phaedra.

Hippomenes (hi-pom′e-nēz) was the conqueror and husband of **Atalanta.**

The **Horae** (hō′rē), or **Hours,** are the Seasons, daughters of Zeus and Themis.

Hyacinth(us) was a youth beloved of **Apollo.**

The **Hyades** (hi′a-dēz) are a constellation. See **Sky Deities.**

The **Hydra** (hi′dra) of Lerna was killed by **Heracles** as the second of his Labors.

Hylas (hi′las), one of the **Argonauts** (see *Outward voyage)*, was drowned in a spring.

Hyllus (hil′us) was a son of **Heracles** and Deianira.

Hymen (hi′men) was the god of marriage.

The **Hyperboreans** (hi-per-bor′ē-anz) were a people living, according to their name, "beyond the north wind." They were favorites of Apollo.

Hyperion (hi-pēr′i-on) was a Titan, and father of Helius, Selene, and Eos. See **Sky Deities.**

Hypermnestra (hi-purm-ncs′tra) was the only one of the **Danaids** who spared her husband.

Hypsipyle (hip-sip′i-lē) was queen of Lemnos. See **Argonauts** *(Outward voyage).*

Iacchus (i-ak′us) was a minor deity connected with the Eleusinian Mysteries (for which see **Hades,** *Persephone*), and sometimes regarded as identical with Bacchus.

Iapetus (i-ap′e-tus), a Titan, was the father of Prometheus.

Icarus (ik′a-rus) was the son of Daedalus. See **Crete.**

Ida (i′da) was the name of two mountains, one near Troy, one in Crete.

Idomeneus (i-dom′e-nūs) was the Cretan leader in the Trojan War.

Ilithyia (i-li-thi′ya), or **Eileithyia,** is goddess of birth, daughter of Zeus and **Hera.**

Ilium (il'i-um) is Troy.

Ilus (i'lus) was an early king of Troy, from whom the city was called Ilium.

Ino (i'nō) was the wife of **Athamas** and the nurse of **Dionysus.**

Io (i'ō), daughter of the river god Inachus, was beloved of Zeus. He visited her, carefully causing a cloud to form above them; but Hera suspected that something was going on under that cloud and brushed it away. Zeus had just changed Io into a beautiful white heifer. He did not quite succeed in allaying Hera's suspicions, for she demanded the heifer as a gift, and then set Argus Panoptes ("the All-seeing"), a powerful giant with one hundred eyes scattered about his body, to watch it. Zeus sent Hermes to free the transformed Io. Hermes lulled Argus to sleep with stories, and, when all hundred eyes had shut, killed him. (An epithet of Hermes is Argiphontes, which by an imaginative stretch of etymological probability the Greeks took to mean "Slayer of Argus." A late intrusion is the detail that Hera scattered the eyes of Argus in the tail of her bird, the peacock.) But now Hera sent another watcher, a gadfly that pursued and stung Io relentlessly, causing her to wander over the face of the earth. She swam the Ionian sea (named for her), crossed the Bosporus (which means "cow pass"), and finally found peace in Egypt. Here she gave birth to a son by Zeus, Epaphus. Among the descendants of Io through Epaphus were the Danaids, Perseus, and Heracles. Io is an important figure in Aeschylus' *Prometheus Bound,* and Ovid tells her story in the *Metamorphoses,* 1.

Iobates (i-ob'a-tēz) was a Lycian king to whom **Bellerophon** was sent.

Iolaus (i-ō-lā'us) was the nephew and companion of Heracles.

Iole (i'ō-lē) was brought home by **Heracles** (*Deianira*) to be his concubine.

Ion (i'on), son of Apollo and Creusa, became king of **Athens.**

Iphicles (if'i-klēz) was the twin brother of **Heracles.**

Iphigenia (if-i-je-ni'a), the daughter of Agamemnon, was sacrificed at Aulis. See **Trojan War** (*Rallying of the host*) and **Atreus.**

Iris (i'ris), goddess of the rainbow and messenger of the gods, was the daughter of two **Sea Deities.**

The **Iron Age** is the last of the **Ages of Man.**

Ismene (iz-mē'nē) was the sister of Antigone, Eteocles, and Polynices, children of Oedipus of **Thebes.**

Ithaca (ith′a-ka), a rocky island west of Greece, was the home of **Odysseus**.

Itylus (it′i-lus), or **Itys** (i′tis), was the son of Procne. See **Athens**.

Iulus (i-ū′lus) is a name of Ascanius, son of **Aeneas** (*Italy*) and Creusa.

Ixion (ik-si′on) is famous for his punishment in the underworld. See **Hades**.   *

Janus (jā′nus) was a Roman deity of some importance. He was the god of entrances and beginnings, and thus was both the guardian of doorways and the helper in the inauguration of all enterprises. He was worshiped especially at the beginning of the year, and the first month of the year, January, was named for him. The door of the temple of Janus in Rome was kept open when Rome was at war, closed in times of peace. He was usually represented as having two heads, or two faces, in order that as god of entrances he might look in both directions.

Jason (jā′son) was the leader of the **Argonauts**.

Jocasta (jō-kas′ta) was the mother and wife of Oedipus of **Thebes**.

Jove (jōv) is Jupiter, the Roman equivalent of **Zeus**.

Juno (jōō′no) is the Roman name of **Hera**.

Jupiter (jōō′pi-ter) is the Roman name of **Zeus**.

The **Labyrinth** (lab′i-rinth) was the home of the Minotaur on Crete. See **Theseus**.

Lachesis (lak′e-sis) was one of the three **Fates**.

Ladon (lā′don) was (1) a serpent who guarded the golden apples of the Hesperides (see **Heracles**, eleventh Labor); (2) a river in Arcadia.

Laertes (lā-ur′tēz) was the father of **Odysseus** (*Ithaca*).

The **Laestrygonians** (les-tri-gō′ni-anz) were cannibal giants encountered by **Odysseus** (*Sea adventures*).

Laius (lā′us) was the father of Oedipus of **Thebes**.

Laocoon (lā-ok′ō-on), priest of Poseidon, died for trying to warn the Trojans against the Wooden Horse. See **Trojan War** (*The fall*).

*read: (ik-sī′on)

Laodamia (lā-ō-da-mi′a) was the wife of **Protesilaus.**

Laomedon (lā-om′e-don) was a king of Troy. See **Heracles** (ninth Labor) and **Trojan War** (*Background*).

The **Lapiths** (lap′iths), or **Lapithae** (lap′i-thē), were a people of Thessaly ruled by Pirithous, friend of **Theseus** (*Later adventures*).

Lares (lar′ēz) and **Penates** are minor Roman deities who protect the household. The Lares are the guardians of the property at large, the Penates the gods of the storeroom. Aeneas was supposed to have brought the original Lares and Penates of the Roman people with him from Troy.

Latinus (la-ti′nus) was king of the Latins in the story of **Aeneas** (*Italy*).

Latona (la-tō′na) is the Roman name of Leto, mother of **Apollo** and Artemis.

Lavinia (la-vin′i-a), daughter of Latinus, was the second wife of **Aeneas** (*Italy*). For her was named

Lavinium (la-vin′i-um), the city founded by **Aeneas** (*Italy*).

Leander (lē-an′der) was the lover of **Hero.**

Leda (lē′da) was the wife of the Laconian hero Tyndareus, a grandson of Aeolus. Zeus fell in love with her and came to her in the form of a swan, in order to escape the notice of Hera. Leda bore four children, two sons, Castor and Polydeuces (Roman Pollux), and two daughters, Helen and Clytemnestra. The precise manner of birth and paternity of these four children is not altogether clear. Usually, some are children of Zeus, some of Tyndareus, some are hatched from eggs, some born normally. Polydeuces and Helen are usually the children of Zeus, Castor and Clytemnestra of Tyndareus. Sometimes Leda lays two eggs, from one of which the two boys are hatched, from the other the two girls. Sometimes there is only one egg; sometimes only Helen is hatched from an egg. One story has it that Helen is daughter of Zeus and Nemesis (a minor and rather abstract divinity, personifying the idea of righteous indignation; for her parentage see under **Chaos**). Nemesis, fleeing the amorous pursuit of Zeus, was turned into a swan, but Zeus turned himself into a swan, too, and overtook Nemesis. Nemesis laid an egg and abandoned it; it was brought to Leda, who hatched it and brought up the baby hatched from it, Helen. The further career of Helen is recorded under **Trojan War,** that of Clytemnestra under **Atreus.**

Castor and Polydeuces are often known as the Dioscuri, the sons of Zeus, sometimes as the Tyndarides, the sons of Tyndareus; in Homer they are both mortal sons of Tyndareus. They appear together with the Argonauts and in the Calydonian Boar Hunt. They rescued Helen when she had been kidnaped by Theseus. The best-known story concerning them is the following. Idas and Lynceus, sons of Aphareus, brother of Leda, were to wed Phoebe and Hilaria, daughters of Leucippus, another brother of Leda. Thus all six were cousins. Castor and Polydeuces kidnaped the two girls at their wedding feast, and were pursued by Idas and Lynceus. Lynceus, who had preternaturally sharp vision, spied the fleeing Dioscuri and their booty halfway across the Peloponnesus and gave chase. There was a fight; Polydeuces killed Lynceus; Idas mortally wounded Castor (the mortal one of the twins) and then was killed by a thunderbolt of Zeus. Rather than have his brother die, Polydeuces shared his immortality with him, and so either they alternate separately, day by day, between heaven and the underworld, or together they spend alternate days in heaven and the underworld.

Castor was a famous charioteer and horseman, Polydeuces a great boxer. Each became the patron deity of his skills.

Two twentieth-century poems about Leda are *Leda and the Swan* (1923), by W. B. Yeats, and *Leda* (1920), by Aldous Huxley. A Roman story of the Dioscuri is told in Macaulay's *The Battle of the Lake Regillus*, one of the *Lays of Ancient Rome* (1842).

Lemnos (lem'nos) is an Aegean island associated with **Hephaestus.** See also **Argonauts** (*Outward voyage*).

Lerna (lur'na), a swamp, was the home of the Lernaean Hydra, killed by **Heracles** as his second Labor.

Lethe (lē'thē), the river of forgetfulness, as its name implies, was one of the rivers of the underworld. See **Hades.**

Leto (lē'tō) was the mother of **Apollo** and Artemis.

Leucothea (lū-coth'ē-a) was Ino, wife of Athamas, after her transformation into a **Sea Deity.**

Liber (li'ber) is a name of **Dionysus.**

Libitina (lib-i-tī'na) was the Roman goddess of death.

Lichas (li'kas) was the herald of Heracles.

Linus (li'nus) was son of Apollo, and a famous musician.

The **Lotus** (lō'tus) **Eaters** were encountered by **Odysseus** and his men at the beginning of their sea adventures.

Lucina (lū-sī'na) is the Roman goddess of childbirth and the daughter of Juno. See **Hera.**

Luna (lōō′na) is Selene, the moon goddess. See **Sky Deities.**

Lyaeus (lī-ē′us) is an epithet of Dionysus. It means the "liberator."

Lycaon (lī-kā′on) was an early king of Arcadia. See **Deucalion.**

Lycurgus (lī-kur′gus) was (1) a king of Nemea, visited by the Seven against **Thebes;** (2) a king of Thrace, punished by **Dionysus.**

Lynceus (lin′sūs) was (1) a son of Aphareus. Noted for his extraordinarily sharp sight, he was an Argonaut, took part in the Calydonian Boar Hunt, and with his brother Idas fought against Castor and Polydeuces. See **Leda.** (2) Husband of the **Danaid** Hypermnestra.

Macaria (ma-kar′i-a), daughter of Heracles, sacrificed herself for her family. See **Heracles** (end of article).

Machaon (ma-kā′on), son of Asclepius, was a physician of the Greek army in the Trojan War.

Maenads (mē′nadz) were the female followers of **Dionysus.**

Maenalus (mē′na-lus), a mountain in Arcadia, was a haunt of Pan.

Maia (mā′a) was the mother by Zeus of **Hermes.**

Manto (man′tō), daughter of Tiresias, was a prophetess.

Marpessa (mar-pes′a), wooed by **Apollo** and Idas, chose Idas.

Mars (marz) is the Roman name of **Ares.**

Marsyas (mar′si-as) was a satyr who challenged **Apollo** to a contest of music.

Medea (me-dē′a), princess of Colchis and sorceress, became wife of Jason of the **Argonauts.**

Medusa (me-dū′sa) was the Gorgon beheaded by **Perseus.** See also **Sea Deities.**

Megaera (me-jē′ra) was one of the Furies. See **Hades** (*Underworld*).

Megara (meg′a-ra) was (1) the first wife of **Heracles** (*Minor stories*); (2) a city ruled by Nisus (see **Athens**).

Melampus (mel-am′pus) was a prophet who helped his brother Bias win Pero (see **Salmoneus**), and cured the daughters of Proetus (see **Dionysus**).

Meleager (mel-ē-ā′jer) is the main hero of the **Calydonian Boar Hunt.**

Melicertes (mel-i-sur′tēz), son of **Athamas** and Ino, became the **Sea Deity** Palaemon.

Melpomene (mel-pom′e-nē) was one of the nine **Muses,** patroness of tragedy.

Memnon (mem′non), son of Eos, was killed by Achilles in the **Trojan War** (*Late events*).

Menelaus (men-e-lā′us) of Sparta, husband of Helen and brother of Agamemnon, was a Greek leader in the **Trojan War.**

Mentor (men′tor) was an adviser of Telemachus in the story of **Odysseus** (*Ithaca*).

Mercury is the Roman name of **Hermes.**

Merope (mĕr′ō-pē) was (1) wife of Cresphontes, mother of Aepytus (see the end of the article **Heracles**); (2) wife of Sisyphus (see **Hades,** *Underworld*) and one of the Pleiades (see **Sky Deities**); (3) beloved of Orion (see **Artemis**).

Metis (mē′tis) was the first wife of **Zeus** and was swallowed by him.

Midas (mī′das) was a Phrygian king about whom two stories are told under **Apollo.**

Milanion (mī-lan′i-on) in some stories was **Atalanta′s** conqueror and husband.

Minerva (mi-nur′va) is the Roman name of **Athena.**

Minos (mī′nos) was the king of **Crete.**

The **Minotaur** (min′o-tawr) was the Cretan monster killed by **Theseus.**

Mnemosyne (nē-mos′i-nē), "Memory," was the mother of the **Muses** by Zeus.

The **Moirae** (moi′rē), or **Moerae** (mē′rē), are the **Fates.**

Moly (mō′lē) was a magic herb that protected **Odysseus** (see *Sea adventures*) against Circe.

Momus (mō'mus), son of Night, was the god of mockery and criticism.

Mopsus (mop'sus) was the name of two prophets: (1) an Argonaut and partici-
pant in the Calydonian Boar Hunt; and (2) a son of Apollo and Manto,
daughter of Tiresias (this Mopsus defeated Calchas in a contest of prophetic
skill).

Morpheus (mor'fūs) was the god of dreams.

Mother-Goddesses, who in some way symbolize or sponsor fertility and pro-
ductiveness in animal and plant life, are more important in religious ritual
than in myth, and what deities of this description there are in Greek myth
usually show a good deal of influence from Near Eastern myth and ritual. The
great mother of all is, of course, Earth (Ge, Gaea, Tellus), for whom see **Earth
and Sky.** Two of her Titan daughters, Themis and Rhea, have some mother-
goddess attributes. Themis is mother, by Zeus, of the Horae, or Seasons,
minor figures symbolizing the annual growth of plant life. Rhea, wife of
Cronus, is often identified with the Phrygian mother-goddess, Cybele, and in
this role she was worshiped with the frenzied and orgiastic ritual that typifies
the worship of fertility deities; her dancing priests are the Corybantes, and
she has a young male consort Attis, as the Egyptian Isis has her consort
Osiris. Rhea Cybele is just on the fringes of Greek and Roman myth. Demeter
(Ceres), the yearly journeyings of whose daughter Persephone, bride of
Hades, represent the annual cycle of vegetation, is the great grain-mother,
sponsor of the growth of crops. **Hera,** though a marriage goddess, has very
little trace of mother-goddess features; there is only the fact that she is sometimes said to be mother of Typhoeus (see **Zeus**). **Aphrodite,** especially in her
love affairs with Adonis and Anchises, for which see under her name, is a
more important figure in this respect. **Artemis** (Diana), usually in myth a
chaste virgin, seems in part of her personality to be connected with a very
early, possibly Minoan, mother figure associated with wild animals, and as
Artemis of Ephesus was apparently worshiped as a goddess of fertility, for
she is represented as a many-breasted mother-goddess, probably under the
influence of similar Near Eastern deities. Semele, mother of Dionysus, who
is sometimes represented as reappearing each spring from below ground, like
Persephone, perhaps has some kinship with a Phrygian mother-goddess.

Mulciber (mul'si-ber) is a Roman name of **Hephaestus.**

Musaeus (mū-zē'us) was a legendary early Greek poet and musician, not the
Musaeus of the sixth century A.D. who wrote about Hero and Leander.

The **Muses** (mū'zez), the nine daughters of Zeus and Mnemosyne ("Memory"),
were the patronesses of literature and inspirers of poets and other practitioners
of the literary arts. In early references there is usually just one Muse, but later

on poetic inspiration was divided into categories, and a Muse was put in charge of each one of nine branches of literature. The assignment of categories varies, but the following is probably the commonest: Calliope the Muse of epic poetry, Clio of history, Euterpe of lyric poetry and flute music, Thalia of comedy, Melpomene of tragedy, Terpsichore of the dance, Erato of love poetry, Polyhymnia of sacred music, and Urania of astronomy. The home of the Muses is about the fountain Hippocrene, on Mount Helicon, in Boeotia, or in the district of Pieria in northern Thessaly, from which they are sometimes called the Pierides. The Muses were, like Apollo with his music, jealous of their prerogative as patronesses of literature, and, like Apollo, they punished those who presumed to rival them. The Thracian minstrel Thamyris, who dared try to outsing them, was struck blind by their power, and his minstrel skill taken away from him. The nine daughters of King Pierus, also called the Pierides, challenged the Muses to a musical contest, were of course defeated, and were turned into magpies. The story is told by Ovid in the *Metamorphoses*, 5.

Mycenae (mī-sē'nē), or Mycene, the city of Atreus and Agamemnon, was the center of the Mycenaean civilization which flourished about 1500–1200 B.C.

Myrmidons (mur'mi-donz) were the troops of Achilles at Troy. For their origin, see **Aeacus.**

Myrrha (mur'a), daughter of **Cinyras,** was the mother of Adonis.

Myrtilus (mur'til-us), the charioteer of Oenomaus, was bribed by **Pelops.**

Naiads (nā'adz) were **nymphs** of springs and rivers.

Narcissus, son of the river god Cephisus and the Naiad Liriope, was an extraordinarily beautiful youth. The nymph Echo fell in love with him. Echo was hampered in her relations with others by reason of a unique peculiarity of speech imposed upon her by Hera. Once upon a time Echo had aided Zeus in a love affair, by keeping Hera occupied in conversation when Hera meant to be checking up on Zeus's activities. As a punishment for such verbal meddling, Hera ordained that henceforth Echo should have no power to initiate conversation, and should be able only to repeat the last words that the most recent speaker had uttered. Thus impeded, Echo had no success in her efforts to rouse Narcissus to an interest in her, and so deeply did she grieve for her unrequited love that she wasted away to nothingness; only the voice, with its strange limitation, was left. But indeed nobody was able to attract Narcissus, and he remained aloof. One day he paused for a drink in a very still forest pool, and beheld in the water his own reflection, though he did not know it. He at once fell in love with the beautiful face that he saw, and now he in his turn pined away in a love that could not be satisfied. At last he was changed into the flower that is named for him. Ovid tells the story in the *Metamorphoses*, 3.

Nausicaa (naw-sik′ā-a), daughter of Alcinous, befriended the shipwrecked **Odysseus** (*Sea adventures*).

Nectar was the drink of the gods.

Neleus (nēl′ūs), son of Tyro and Poseidon, was the father of Nestor and Pero. See **Salmoneus** and **Heracles** (*Minor stories*).

Nemea (nem′ē-a) is a valley in the Peloponnesus where **Heracles** slew the Nemean (ne-mē′an) lion (first Labor), and where an incident of the Seven against **Thebes** took place.

Nemesis (nem′e-sis), daughter of Night, was the goddess of righteous indignation. She is sometimes said to be mother of Helen. See **Leda.**

Neoptolemus (nē-op-tol′e-mus), who is also called Pyrrhus, was the son of Achilles, and the chief sacker of Troy in the Trojan War.

Neptune (nep′tūn) is the Roman name of **Poseidon.**

The **Nereids** (nē′rē-idz) were the fifty daughters of Nereus. See **Sea Deities.**

Nereus (nēr′ūs) was one of the **Sea Deities.**

Nessus (nes′us) was a centaur who attempted to violate Deianira and was killed by **Heracles.**

Nestor (nes′tor) was the eldest of the Greek leaders in the **Trojan War.**

Night was daughter of **Chaos.**

Niobe (ni′ō-bē) of **Thebes** was punished by Apollo and Artemis for boasting of her children.

Nisus (ni′sus) (1) took part in a night raid with Euryalus in the story of **Aeneas** (*Italy*); (2) was king of Megara (see **Athens**).

Notus (nō′tus) is the south wind. See **Wind Deities.**

The **Nymphs** were minor deities associated with and having some power over certain kinds of localities: springs and rivers, trees and woods, mountains, and the sea. The Naiads were water nymphs associated with springs and rivers; the Oceanids (daughters of Oceanus) and the Nereids (daughters of Nereus, see under **Sea Deities**) were associated with the sea; the Oreads were mountain nymphs; the Dryads and Hamadryads were tree nymphs, sometimes supposed to live only as long as the particular tree with which they were associated lived. Ovid tells how a young mother named Dryope ∗ became a Dryad after her infant had broken off a leaf of Lotis, the Dryad of a lotus tree; in retaliation Dryope was transformed on the spot into a lotus tree and became the Dryad of the tree.

Oceanids (ō-sē′a-nidz), daughters of Oceanus, were ocean **nymphs.**

Oceanus (ō-sē′a-nus), a **Titan,** is the god of the stream surrounding the earth.

Odysseus (ō-dis′ūs), called Ulysses by the Romans, whose deeds of prowess and craft at the siege of Troy are described under **Trojan War,** spent ten years of wandering, after the fall of Troy, before he regained his home in the island of Ithaca, off the west coast of Greece. Brave, cunning, resourceful, and resilient, he is the ideal hero of adventure. He is the darling of Athena, who helps him and admires his skill in lying. Instead of following the structure of the *Odyssey,* we shall outline Odysseus' adventures in chronological order from the fall of Troy.

Sea adventures. Setting out from Troy with his contingent of twelve ships, Odysseus landed first in the region of the Cicones, in Thrace, and there raided the city of Ismarus, losing six men from each ship. He spared Maro, priest of Apollo, and was rewarded by the gift of some marvelous wine, later very useful to him. Next, after being blown hopelessly off course, they came to the land of the Lotus-Eaters, and from this point until Ithaca is reached the geography is merely a Mediterranean fairyland. The Lotus-Eaters offered no violence to Odysseus' men but gave them the lotus plant to eat. Some of the men ate of it, and forgot home and family; they wanted to do nothing ever after but sit and dream and eat the lotus. Odysseus had to have those affected dragged back to the ships and confined below decks.

The next adventure is the most famous, and, as told in the *Odyssey,* has a fair claim to be regarded as the most perfect of all stories of fantastic adventure. Odysseus and twelve men go ashore and find a huge cave, giving evidence of a gigantic inhabitant. They await the owner's return, and in the evening a one-eyed giant enters the cave, driving in his flock of giant sheep. It is Polyphemus, the Cyclops. Spying the men, he seizes two of them and devours them raw for his evening meal, bars the door with a huge stone, and sleeps. In the morning, after a breakfast of two more men, he bars the door and takes his sheep to pasture. Odysseus devises a scheme of revenge and escape. He and his men sharpen to a point one end of a great staff that

---

*read: Ovid, *Metamorphoses* I,

they find lying in the cave. With evening comes the Cyclops, and then his dinner; now Odysseus and six others are left. Odysseus offers the Cyclops some of the powerful wine from Ismarus, and Polyphemus, not accustomed to any beverage but milk, becomes very drunk. After a conversation in which Odysseus tells him that his name is No-man, the giant falls into a drunken sleep. Then the men heat the pointed staff to a red glow, and plunge it into the one monstrous eye of the Cyclops. Blinded, he roars for help. Other Cyclopes come and from outside the cave ask who it is that is attacking him. When Polyphemus answers "No-man," they all leave.

In the morning, Polyphemus rolls the stone away to let his flock out to pasture, and feels the back of each sheep as it leaves, in case the men should try to escape on the backs of the sheep. But crafty Odysseus has tied the men to the bellies of the sheep, and they get away, Odysseus last of all, clinging beneath the pet ram of the Cyclops. They make their way to the shore and gain their ship, and then Odysseus makes a mistake: he tauntingly reveals his name to the Cyclops, who calls upon his father Poseidon to punish his tormentor. He prays that Odysseus may never reach home, or, if he must, that he arrive there late, without his men, in a foreign ship, and that he find troubles at home. Poseidon fulfills his son's second prayer.

More difficulties follow. They come to the island of the king of the winds, Aeolus, son of Hippotas (see also under **Wind Deities**), who entertains them kindly and gives Odysseus a bag containing all the winds but the west wind, which will drive them home. When they are in sight of Ithaca the men begin to suspect that the bag holds some treasure of which they are unjustly deprived. They open the bag. Out rush the winds, a storm ensues, and they are driven right back to Aeolus, who this time angrily sends them away without help. Then they come to the land of the Laestrygonians, man-eating giants who catch two men and, when the rest regain their ships, hurl great stones and destroy all the ships, with their companies, except that of Odysseus. Odysseus had cautiously moored his vessel outside the harbor.

The one remaining ship arrives at Aeaea, the island where dwells the sorceress Circe, daughter of Helius and thus sister of Medea's father, Aeetes. Odysseus sends half his company, under Eurylochus, to explore. They come to the palace of Circe, who lavishly entertains all of them except Eurylochus, who refuses to enter. Then she transforms the men into swine and drives them off to a sty. Eurylochus takes the sad news back, and now Odysseus sets out alone. On his way he meets Hermes, who tells him how to deal with Circe and gives him a magic root called moly, to protect him against Circe's enchantments. Thus equipped, Odysseus gains mastery over Circe, who retransforms the men and entertains the whole company for a year.

After this long pause they sail on, to the land of the Cimmerians in the far west, a region of mist and darkness. Near here is access to the underworld, where Odysseus goes to ask Tiresias, the great Theban prophet, now in the underworld, how they can reach home. Here Odysseus sees, besides

Tiresias, the shades of numerous illustrious dead: Ajax, who, still angry over the judgment of the armor (see **Trojan War,** *Late events*), refuses to speak to him; Achilles; many of the famous sinners (for whose punishments see under **Hades,** *Underworld*); and a number of famous beauties. After this strange visit, Odysseus and his men return to Circe, and then proceed on their way. Their next peril is the island of the Sirens, two bird-women who lure ships to destruction on the rocks by the irresistible enchantment of their singing. Eager to hear their voices without disaster, Odysseus melts wax and fastens it in the ears of his men, has them bind him to the mast, and charges them to pay no attention to his nods and gestures until they are clear of the area. And so Odysseus' curiosity is satisfied. From there they make their way between Scylla, the monster with a ring of ravening hounds about her waist, in a lair on one side of a narrow strait, and on the other side Charybdis, even more terrifying, who sucks whole ships into her greedy maw. (The identification of Scylla and Charybdis with the Straits of Messina may well be quite late.) Sailing closer to Scylla, Odysseus gets through, with the loss of six men.

Finally they come to Thrinacia, an island on which is pastured a herd of cattle belonging to the Sun. Held here for a whole month by adverse winds, and in need of food, Odysseus' men, against their leader's command, kill and eat several of the cattle while Odysseus is asleep. Soon they are able to leave the island, but before long their impiety in devouring the cattle is punished when the ship is blasted by a thunderbolt and all the men but Odysseus perish.

Odysseus makes his way, clinging to a spar, through the same perilous strait as before, narrowly escaping Charybdis this time. He ultimately reaches the island of Ogygia, where lives the lovely nymph Calypso. For seven years Odysseus remains the prisoner and husband of Calypso, who wishes him to stay permanently and offers him immortality if he will do so. But Odysseus longs for home and his wife Penelope, and finally, at Athena's insistence, Zeus sends Hermes to bid Calypso let Odysseus go. He builds a crude boat and sails away, only to be wrecked by Poseidon, in a last act of hostility. Rescued by Leucothea (for whom see under **Sea Deities,** end of article), who gives him a magic girdle to hold him up, Odysseus reaches land, more dead than alive, and finds himself on the island of Scheria, where the Phaeacians dwell. He is discovered there by Nausicaa, the daughter of King Alcinous, is kindly entertained by the Phaeacians, and tells them the story of his adventures. Finally they take him to Ithaca in one of their ships, and land him at a hidden corner of the island.

Ithaca. The rest of the story of Odysseus is more fiction than myth, and though it is a rousing and satisfying tale, it must be passed over very briefly here. After being landed on Ithaca in a deep sleep, Odysseus wakes up in confusion as to where he is and what he is to do. Athena comes to him and advises him, at the same time disguising him as an old beggar. In this disguise he makes his way to the hut of his swineherd, Eumaeus. After an encounter in which he is nearly finished off by Eumaeus's dogs, Odysseus is kindly received by the faithful servant. Soon after, Odysseus' son Telemachus comes to the hut, having just returned to Ithaca from a visit to Nestor at Pylos, and Menelaus and Helen at Sparta, whither he had gone in search of news of his father. He had been urged to this and helped in it by Athena, disguised as Mentor, an old friend of Odysseus who had been left in charge of Odysseus' property during his absence.

Ithaca had fallen on evil days in the long years of Odysseus' wanderings. Everyone thought that he had died, and numerous princes of Ithaca and the neighboring territories had come to sue for the hand of Penelope. For three years Penelope had put them off, pretending that she would choose among them when she had finished weaving a burial garment for old Laertes, father of Odysseus. Each night she would secretly undo what she had woven during the day, until finally a faithless handmaid betrayed the trick, whereupon the suitors became more insistent. While they waited, they devoured the goods of Odysseus in feasting, and treated his household with insolent disregard.

At the hut of Eumaeus, Odysseus and Telemachus are united, and plan revenge on the suitors. Odysseus, still in disguise, goes to the palace. He is recognized by his old hunting hound, Argus, a fleet young hunter when he left, but now lying neglected in the stable yard. Argus wags his tail feebly in joy, recognizing his disguised master, and then dies. Odysseus boxes and soundly trounces a large and insolent beggar named Irus. Biding his time, he endures the arrogant behavior of the suitors. He speaks to Penelope, but does not reveal himself, though his old nurse, Euryclea, recognizes him when she bathes his feet and sees an old scar on his leg. Finally, in a contest to see who can string the bow of Odysseus, only the old beggar who is Odysseus succeeds. Then he turns his arrows against the suitors and kills them, beginning with Antinous, the most arrogant of them all and their leader. With the aid of Telemachus, Eumaeus, and one other faithful servant, together with Athena, Odysseus completes his revenge against suitors and unfaithful servants. Then he reveals himself to Penelope, who will not accept him as Odysseus until he shows his knowledge of a secret shared by them alone: that their bed is built of the trunk of a still rooted tree and hence is immovable. Finally, by divine intervention, peace is established between the victorious Odysseus and the angry families of the slain suitors.

The familiar, Homeric story of Odysseus ends at this point. There are various continuations, some of them faintly suggested by the *Odyssey*. The best-known additional episode tells how in later years, Telegonus, son of Odysseus by Circe, came to Ithaca looking for his father, and accidentally killed him by an arrow wound. Then Telegonus took Penelope and Telemachus back to Circe's isle, where Telegonus married Penelope, and Telemachus married Circe. But Penelope is also reported to have been seduced by the suitor Antinous, and for this to have been sent home by Odysseus to her father, Icarius; later she is said to have gone to Arcadia, and there to have borne Pan to Hermes. But these gossipy postscripts bear no real relation to the characters or careers of Odysseus and his family.

In addition to the *Odyssey*, Odysseus is prominent in two ancient plays, Sophocles' *Ajax* and *Philoctetes*. Dante adds a new chapter to Odysseus' story in the *Divine Comedy, Inferno*, 26. Tennyson's best short poem, *Ulysses* (1842), owes something to Dante and to Homer; Tennyson describes an Odyssean incident in the *Lotos-Eaters* (1842). Several plays have been written on the Odysseus theme, among them Stephen Phillips's *Ulysses* (1902). The profundity of James Joyce's debt to Homer in *Ulysses* may be questioned, but that the general framework and much symbolism depend on it is beyond doubt. A modern Greek epic is Nikos Kazantzakis' *Odyssey* (1936, English translation, 1958), which is a continuation of Homer's poem more than twice its length. For the literary history of the story of Odysseus, see W. B. Stanford, *The Ulysses Theme* (1954).

Oedipus (ē'di-pus) of **Thebes** killed his father and married his mother.

Oeneus (ē'nūs) was king of Calydon (see **Calydonian Boar Hunt**).

Oenomaus (ē-nō-mā'us), king of Pisa and father of Hippodamia, was overcome by **Pelops.**

Oenone (ē-nō'nē), a nymph, was the wife of Paris before the time of the **Trojan War.** See Tennyson's *Oenone* (1842).

Oeta (ē'ta) is the mountain in Thessaly where **Heracles** was cremated.

Ogyges (ō-ji'jēz) is the name of a very early king of Thebes and of a very early king of Athens.

Ogygia (ō-jij'i-a) is Calypso's isle. See **Odysseus** (*Sea adventures*).

Olympia (ō-lim'pi-a), in the northwest part of the Peloponnesus, was the site of the Olympic Games.

Olympus (ō-lim'pus) is a mountain in northern Greece on which the gods dwelt.

Omphale (om'fa-lē), queen of Lydia, had **Heracles** (see *Minor stories*) as her slave for a year.

Ops (ops) was a Roman goddess of agriculture and wife of Saturn.

Orcus (or'kus) is a name of **Hades.**

Oreads (or'ē-adz) are mountain **nymphs.**

Orestes (o-res'tēz) was the son and avenger of Agamemnon (see **Atreus**).

Orion (ō-rī'on), a giant and a hunter, was carried off by Eos (see **Sky Deities**) and later was killed by **Artemis.**

Orithyia (or-i-thi'ya), daughter of Erechtheus of **Athens,** was the wife of Boreas.

Orpheus (or'fūs), son of the Muse Calliope, either by a Thracian king, Oeagrus, or by Apollo, was the greatest of all musicians. So great was his skill in singing and playing the lyre that he could enchant not only men and animals but even the very stones and trees of the Thracian mountains in which he dwelt. He was one of the Argonauts, and on their voyage performed various feats of musical skill, as when he saved the Argonauts from the Sirens by distracting the men from their song with his own more winning music. He married the nymph Eurydice, but on the very day of their wedding or soon thereafter, Eurydice, pursued by the lustful Aristaeus, a minor agricultural deity, in her precipitate flight stepped on a snake and died of its bite. Orpheus made his way alive to the realm of Hades and by the eloquence of his minstrel plea gained the privilege of leading Eurydice back to the world of light. But the condition was made that he must not look back at her until they were clear of the underworld regions. Just at the cavernous portal of the underworld, the impetuous lover looked back too soon, and Eurydice faded from his sight. Orpheus wandered sadly about the Thracian woods, contemning all human contact, and thus rousing the hostility of the Thracian women, who tore him to pieces in a Dionysiac frenzy. His head and lyre, thrown into the river Hebrus, floated to the island of Lesbos.

Some stories of Orpheus go beyond mythology into the realm of religious and pseudohistorical tradition. There are various hymns extant which were in antiquity ascribed to Orpheus; all are of course forgeries, and none even very old. He was said to have invented the mysteries of Dionysus, and there was perhaps even a sect, the Orphics, named for him. But the nature and even the existence of the sect are dubious. The tradition according to which Dionysus was torn to pieces and eaten by the Titans is associated with Orpheus.

The best ancient rendering, and likely the best of all renderings, is in Virgil's *Georgics*, 4. See also Ovid's *Metamorphoses*, 10. Orpheus has, naturally enough, been a favorite of musicians; among operas on the story are those of Monteverdi and Gluck. Among poems may be mentioned the Middle English *Sir Orfeo* and Shelley's *Orpheus* (1820); among plays, two recent French interpretations, Jean Anouilh's *Eurydice* and Jean Cocteau's *Orphée*.

Ortygia (or-tij'i-a), an island, part of Syracuse, Sicily, was the second home of Arethusa and Alpheus. See **Sea Deities.**

Ossa (os′a), a mountain of Thessaly, was used by Otus and Ephialtes in their attack on the gods. See **Zeus.**

Otus (ō′tus) was a giant who, with his brother Ephialtes, attacked the gods. See **Zeus.**

Paean (pē′an) is a name of Apollo. It means the "healer."

Palaemon (pa-lē′mon) is a minor **Sea Deity,** son of **Athamas** and Ino.

Palamedes (pal-a-mē′dēz) was famous as an inventor and a wise man. He was done to death by Odysseus in the **Trojan War** (*Rallying of the host, early events*).

Pales (pā′lēz) was an Italian pastoral goddess.

Palinurus (pal-i-nū′rus) was a helmsman of Aeneas who was lost at sea.

The **Palladium** (pa-lā′di-um) was a wooden statue of Athena in Troy, which protected the city as long as it remained there. For its theft from Troy, see **Trojan War** (*The fall*). In Matthew Arnold's *Palladium* (1867) the soul is man's Palladium.

Pallas (pal′as) was (1) an epithet of Athena; (2) a giant; (3) son of Evander, the ally of **Aeneas** (*Italy*); (4) husband of **Styx.**

Pan, Roman Faunus, son of Hermes, is the woodland god of Arcadia, patron of shepherds and their flocks. He is represented as part man, part goat, usually with ears, tail, and hind legs of a goat. He is thus like the satyrs and sileni of Dionysus, and is sometimes said to be father of Silenus. He is often associated with Dionysiac revels. He is playful, lascivious, and unpredictable, sometimes inspiring groups with a sudden "panic" fear. He is a musician too, his instrument being the reed pipe beloved of shepherds. His musical contest with **Apollo** is recorded under that god's name.

He is the lover and pursuer of many nymphs. One of these was Syrinx. Before Pan could overtake her, she was transformed into a bed of reeds. Pan cut from the reeds the first Pan-pipe, which in Greek is *syrinx*. Pitys was another nymph who fled his amorous approach. She was turned into a pine tree. Still a third nymph, Echo, fled from Pan; in revenge, he inspired a group of shepherds with panic and caused them to tear the nymph to pieces. Only her voice was left. (The commoner story of Echo is told under **Narcissus.**)

When the great Athenian runner, Phidippides, who ran from Athens to Sparta and back at the time of the battle of Marathon, was traversing Arcadia on his return, he encountered Pan, who offered his aid to the Athenians if they would institute his worship in their city. This was the beginning of the worship of Pan in Athens.

The death of Pan is a motif of late antiquity and later literature connected with the rise of Christianity. Whatever the origin of the idea, it symbolizes the fading of the influence of pagan deities.

Poems on Pan are more numerous than distinguished; suffice it to cite Keats's *Endymion*, 1. 232–306 (1818), Shelley's *Hymn of Pan* (1820), and Swinburne's *A Nympholept* (1894). See also *The Story of a Panic*, in *The Collected Tales of E. M. Forster* (1947).

Pandar(us) (pan'dar-[us]), a minor figure in the Trojan War, is famous as the go-between in the medieval story of Troilus and Cressida. See **Trojan War** (*Early events*).

Pandion (pan-di'on) is the name of one or two kings of **Athens.**

Pandora (pan-dor'a), the woman of all gifts, as her name suggests, was sent to earth by Zeus as a punishment for Prometheus' theft of fire. She was molded by Hephaestus, endowed by all the gods with various charms and wiles, and brought down by Hermes. The rest of her story is told in two different versions. In one, she brought with her a jar, which was accepted as a gift from the gods by Epimetheus, brother of Prometheus. When Pandora lifted the lid from the jar, there flew from it myriad plagues and evils, which forever wander among mankind. When by the will of Zeus the lid was replaced, only Hope remained trapped within the jar. The meaning of the trapping or retention of Hope is not explained in the original version of the story in Hesiod, and later writers have varied in interpreting whether Hope is thus held for or from man. The other version is a misogynistic story. There is no jar, and Pandora herself is the evil. She is the ancestress of woman: "From her is the race of women, who dwell among mortal men as a great bane" (Hesiod, *Theogony*, 590–592).

Panope (pan'o-pē) was a Nereid.

Paphos (pā'fos) was a city in Cyprus, famed as a center of the worship of Aphrodite.

The **Parcae** (par'sē) are the **Fates.**

Paris (par'is), son of Priam, was the abductor of Helen after his famous Judgment. See **Trojan War.**

Parnassus (par-nas'us) is a mountain in central Greece. On its slopes are Delphi, where **Apollo's** oracular shrine was situated, and Castalia, a spring of the Muses.

Parthenopaeus (par-then-ō-pē'us), son of Atalanta, was one of the Seven against **Thebes.**

Parthenope (par-then′ō-pē) was one of the Sirens.

Pasiphae (pa-sif′a-ē) was the wife of Minos of **Crete,** and mother of the Minotaur.

Patroclus (pa-trō′klus) was the beloved friend of Achilles in the Trojan War.

Pegasus (peg′a-sus) was a winged horse, son of Medusa and Poseidon. See **Bellerophon.**

Peleus (pēl′ūs), son of Aeacus and father of Achilles, is in many stories. See the references given under **Aeacus.**

Pelias (pē′li-as), son of Poseidon and Tyro (see **Salmoneus**) and king of Thessaly, appears in the story of the **Argonauts.**

Pelion (pē′li-on), a mountain in Thessaly, was used by Otus and Ephialtes in their attack on the gods. See **Zeus.**

Pelops (pē′lops), son of Tantalus, king of Phrygia, survived, by divine intervention, the incident in which his father served him as food to the gods (see **Hades,** *Underworld*). While still a youth he went to the Peloponnesus, of which he is the eponymous hero. He made his way to the realm of Oenomaus, king of Pisa, whose daughter Hippodamia was offered as bride to whoever could survive a demanding test. The prospective bridegroom was required to drive away in a chariot with his bride; Oenomaus would pursue in his chariot, and if he overtook the fleeing chariot the young man would receive his spear in the back. Oenomaus was a keen and proficient chariot driver and an accurate spearsman, so that when Pelops arrived on the scene Hippodamia was still unwed, though twelve or thirteen suitors had tried. Pelops bribed Oenomaus' charioteer, Myrtilus, son of Hermes, to help him by removing a linchpin from a wheel of Oenomaus' chariot and replacing it with a wax pin. When the chariot ran, the wax pin melted and broke, causing Oenomaus to suffer a fatal spill. (In one version it is Hippodamia, in love with Pelops, who prevails on Myrtilus, who is in love with her.) Pelops later threw Myrtilus into the sea, either because he was a rival for Hippodamia or simply to clear the air. But as he died Myrtilus cursed Pelops and his descendants, and through his divine father Hermes the curse was brought to fulfillment. Pelops succeeded to the throne of Oenomaus, and he and Hippodamia had as sons Atreus and Thyestes. For further adventures of the family, see **Atreus.**

The **Penates** (pe-nā′tēz) were Roman household gods. See **Lares.**

Penelope (pe-nel′ō-pē) was the wife of **Odysseus.**

Peneus (pe-nē'us) was (1) a river god, father of Daphne (see **Apollo**); (2) a river used by **Heracles** in cleaning the Augean stables (sixth Labor).

Penthesilea (pen-thes-i-lē'a) was queen of the Amazons in the **Trojan War** (*Late events*).

Pentheus (pen'thūs), king of Thebes, was a victim of **Dionysus**.

Persephone (pur-sef'ō-nē), daughter of Demeter, was the wife of **Hades**.

Perseus (pur'sūs) was the son of Zeus and Danae. His story might stand as a model of the career of a hero. King Acrisius of Argos, warned by prophecy that a son born of his daughter Danae would kill him, shut Danae away in a brazen tower or underground chamber. There Zeus beheld her, fell in love with her, and came to her, through the narrow window of her chamber, as a shower of gold. Thus impregnated, Danae gave birth to a son, Perseus. Acrisius' next move was to enclose Danae and the infant in a chest, which he set afloat on the sea. The chest floated to the island of Seriphus and was there found by a fisherman named Dictys, who rescued the mother and child and gave them shelter. There Perseus grew to young manhood.

Meanwhile, Polydectes, brother of Dictys and king of Seriphus, bestowed upon Danae unwelcome attentions. Thinking that his suit would be easier without the virile young Perseus around to protect his mother, Polydectes sent the youth off on a quest. He was to bring back the head of Medusa, one of the Gorgons, three sisters of hideous appearance, winged, their heads wreathed with serpents instead of hair, with the strange power of turning to stone whoever looked upon their faces. Perseus was aided in his quest by Athena and Hermes. Athena gave him her shield, and Hermes guided him to the cave where dwelt the three Graeae ("Gray Ones"), sisters of the Gorgons, women who were gray from birth, and who had among them just one tooth and one eye. Perseus seized the communal tooth and eye and would not give them back until the Graeae told him how to get to the home of certain nymphs who had the equipment he needed to perform his task: a cap of invisibility, winged sandals to enable him to fly, and a wallet in which to put the head of Medusa. Having obtained these, Perseus flew to the cave of the Gorgons, and there found the three of them, Stheno, Euryale, and Medusa, asleep. He approached Medusa without looking directly at her; looking, instead, at her reflection in the burnished shield of Athena, he was able to cut off her head, which he did with a curved sickle provided by Hermes. Clapping the head of Medusa into the wallet, off flew Perseus on his winged sandals. The two sister Gorgons awoke and gave chase, but, rendered invisible by the magic cap, Perseus easily escaped.

Perseus' return trip was eventful. He flew past Atlas, and when the giant offered violence (Atlas suspected that Perseus was after the golden apples, because he knew that a son of Zeus would come for them; but it was another son; see further under **Heracles,** eleventh Labor) Perseus turned him to stone by showing him the Gorgon's head. Later, on a remote sea-coast, Perseus beheld a beautiful girl chained to a rock by the water's edge. On inquiry, he found that this was Andromeda, daughter of King Cepheus and Queen Cassiopeia. Andromeda was being sacrificed to a terrible sea monster, which Poseidon in anger had sent to ravage the land, and which could be appeased only by the sacrifice of the king's daughter. Poseidon's anger was caused by Cassiopeia, who had boasted that she (in some versions, her daughter) excelled the very sea nymphs in beauty. Perseus fell in love with Andromeda, and undertook to rescue her by slaying the dragon, stipulating that if successful he should be rewarded by her hand in marriage. The dragon duly came and was dispatched by Perseus, either by the sword or by the power of Medusa's head. Perseus was about to claim his bride when a certain Phineus, a former suitor, came forward and claimed Andromeda on the strength of her prior commitment to him. Perseus' case was clearly superioï, since Phineus had abandoned Andromeda to her fate, but Phineus and his followers undertook to fight the matter out, and were promptly turned to stone.

Perseus, taking Andromeda with him, now returned to Seriphus, where Polydectes was still harassing Danae. Polydectes was dispatched by Perseus by the now customary process of petrifaction, and Dictys was established as king of Seriphus. Perseus and Danae returned to Argos, and on hearing of their approach Acrisius fled to Thessaly. But he could not escape his fate. Later on, when Perseus was participating in athletic contests in Thessaly, he threw the discus beyond the target area, accidentally struck a spectator, and killed him. The spectator was Acrisius. Perseus became ruler of Tiryns, and among the children of Perseus and Andromeda were Alcaeus, father of Amphitryon, and Electryon, father of Alcmena. The head of Medusa Perseus gave to Athena, who placed it in the middle of her shield or aegis.

For its fame as a myth, the story of Perseus has attracted remarkably little attention from poets. There are no great ancient versions of it extant. It can be found, as nearly everything can, in Ovid's *Metamorphoses* (4 and 5), but it is far from being one of Ovid's best stories. In that other place where nearly everything can be found, William Morris's *The Earthly Paradise* (1868), *The Doom of King Acrisius* is one of the best stories. Also worth mentioning is Charles Kingsley's *Andromeda* (1858).

The **Phaeacians** (fē-ā'shanz) were a people visited by **Odysseus** (*Sea adventures*).

Phaedra (fē'dra), wife of **Theseus,** fell in love with her stepson, Hippolytus.

Phaethon (fā'e-thon), son of the sun god, was killed when he drove his father's chariot. See **Sky Deities.**

Philemon (fi-lē'mon) and **Baucis** were a poor but good and hospitable old couple who entertained Zeus and Hermes with such warm, though humble, hospitality that they were rewarded by the gods by being made priest and priestess of a temple. On their death they were transformed into intertwining trees. Ovid tells the story well in the *Metamorphoses*, 8, and Swift has a delightful parody of it, *Baucis and Philemon* (1706).

Philoctetes (fil-ok-tē'tēz), a hero of the **Trojan War** (end of *Rallying of the host; Late events*), was exiled on Lemnos for ten years.

Philomel(a) (fil'ō-mel, fil-ō-mē'la) was the sister of Procne. See **Athens.**

Philyra (fil'i-ra), according to some versions, was mother, by **Cronus,** of the centaur Chiron.

Phineus (fin'ūs) was (1) husband of Cleopatra and Idaea (see **Athens**), and appears in the story of the **Argonauts** (*Outward voyage*); (2) a suitor of Andromeda (see **Perseus**).

Phlegethon (fleg'e-thon) or Pyriphlegethon, "the fiery river," is a river of the underworld. See **Hades.**

Phlegra (fleg'ra) was the site of the battle of the gods and the Giants. See **Zeus.**

Phoebe (fē'bē) was (1) a name of Artemis; (2) a Titan; (3) a daughter of Leucippus (see **Leda**).

Phoebus (fē'bus) is **Apollo.**

Phoenix (fē'nix) was an aged friend of Achilles in the **Trojan War** (*Iliad*), and his former tutor. In his youth Phoenix had, at his mother's urging, stolen from his father Amyntor the affections of his mistress. In anger, Amyntor blinded Phoenix and sent him into exile. Phoenix became a henchman of Peleus and had his sight restored by the centaur Chiron.

The **Phoenix** (fē'nix) was a fabulous bird of giant size and great beauty, which lived for hundreds of years and was finally cremated. From its ashes another Phoenix arose, or the same one sprang again, resuscitated.

Phrixus (frik'sus), son of **Athamas,** went to Colchis on a gold-fleeced ram. See **Argonauts** (*Background*).

Picus (pī'kus) was the woodpecker, the bird sacred to Mars. He was also said to have been the first king of Latium, the province of Italy in which Rome is situated, and to have been father of the woodland deity Faunus, who much resembles the Greek Pan. Picus was turned into a woodpecker by the sorceress Circe, who fell in love with him and punished him by transformation when he, remaining faithful to the nymph Canens, refused to return her affection.

Pieria (pī-ēr′i-a) was a district in Thessaly where the **Muses** dwelt.

Pierides (pī-er′i-dēz) are the Muses or the daughters of Pierus. See **Muses.**

Pirithous (pi-rith′ō-us) was king of the Lapiths and friend of **Theseus** (*Later adventures*).

The **Pleiades** (plē′a-dēz) were nymphs who became stars. See **Sky Deities.**

Pluto (plōō′tō) is **Hades.**

Plutus (plōō′tus) is the god of wealth, probably in origin the same as Pluto. See **Hades.**

Podalirius (pō-da-lī′ri-us), son of Asclepius, was a physician of the Greeks in the Trojan War.

Pollux (pol′ux) was **Polydeuces.**   *

Polydeuces (pol-i-dū′sēz) was the twin of Castor and the son of **Leda.**

Polydorus (pol-i-dō′rus), son of Priam, was murdered by Polymestor. See **Aeneas** (*Wanderings*).

Polyhymnia (pol-i-him′ni-a) was one of the nine **Muses,** patroness of sacred music.

Polymestor (pol-i-mes′tor), a Thracian king, murdered Polydorus. See **Aeneas** (*Wanderings*).

Polynices (pol-i-nī′sēz), son of Oedipus, raised the expedition of the Seven against **Thebes.**

Polyphemus (pol-i-fē′mus) was the Cyclops encountered by **Odysseus** (*Sea adventures*). See also the story of Galatea, under **Sea Deities.**

Polyxena (po-lik′se-na), daughter of Priam, was sacrificed at the end of the **Trojan War.**

Pomona (pō-mō′na), a goddess of fruit, was beloved of **Vertumnus.**

*read: was the Roman name of **Polydeuces.**

Poseidon (pō-sī'don), Roman Neptune, son of Cronus and Rhea, is the principal god of the sea. (For others, see **Sea Deities.**) He is represented as a mature but vigorous bearded male, like his brother Zeus but less majestic and sedate. He is somewhat more kingly as Neptune than as Poseidon. He bears the trident, which is like a three-pronged fish spear. He is the god of earthquakes as well as the sea, and is called both Earth-holder and Earth-shaker. He is also specially connected with horses, and has frequent association with sundry giants and monsters. There is an undercurrent of violence about many of his activities. It is he who sends a bull from the sea against Hippolytus (**Theseus**), dragons to devour Andromeda (**Perseus**) and Hesione (**Heracles**), and sea serpents to punish Laocoon (**Trojan War**).

His domestic life is rather tame. His wife, Amphitrite, is not much of a figure in myth; neither is their son Triton, who is generally represented as a merman, and is mainly distinguished for his skill in sounding the conch. Poseidon's love affairs, however, are generally in some way violent. He mates with Medusa, whose resultant offspring are Chrysaor and Pegasus (see under **Sea Deities**). In the form of a stallion he mates with Demeter in the form of a mare; the offspring of the union is a talking horse, Arion, the steed of Adrastus of the Seven against Thebes. He is father of the Cyclops Polyphemus (see **Odysseus,** *Sea adventures*), and of the impious giants Otus and Ephialtes (see **Zeus**). His children by the beautiful Tyro, daughter of Salmoneus, were more normal; they were the twins Pelias, uncle of Jason of the Argonauts, and Neleus, father of Nestor of the Trojan War. Glaucus and Proteus, who are sometimes regarded as sons of Poseidon, are dealt with under **Sea Deities.**

There is a well-known story of how he and Athena decided by a contest of benefaction who should be patron deity of Athens. Poseidon struck the rock of the Acropolis with his trident and a horse (or in some versions a spring of salt water) sprang up. Athena touched the ground with her spear and an olive tree forthwith grew on the spot. Athena was adjudged the winner.

Priam (prī'am) was king of Troy during the **Trojan War.**

Priapus (prī-ā'pus) was a minor deity particularly associated with gardens, both as a sponsor of fertility and as a scarecrow. He was regularly adorned prominently with the phallus. He is commonly a figure of fun, associated with somewhat obscene humor. He was sometimes regarded as a son of Dionysus and Aphrodite.

Procne (prok'nē) was the sister of Philomela. See **Athens.**

Procris (prō'kris) was the wife of Cephalus. See **Athens.**

Procrustes (prō-krus'tēz) forced his guests to fit his bed. He was killed by **Theseus** (*Early adventures*).

Progne (prog'nē) is **Procne.**

Prometheus (prō-mē'thūs), whose name the Greeks took to mean the "Fore-thinker," was son of the Titan Iapetus (his mother being either Themis or Asia), and is usually himself referred to as a Titan. He is the champion of *
man, and the antagonist of Zeus on man's behalf, though he had been the ally of Zeus in the battle of the gods against the Titans (see **Zeus**). Ovid and other relatively late writers say that he molded man from clay; in the greatest of all ancient treatments of the myth, Aeschylus' play, *Prometheus Bound*, many of the arts of civilization are said to have been given by him. The one gift always associated with him is fire, which he stole from heaven in a fennel stock and brought to earth. For this deed he was punished by Zeus, who already had a grudge against him, according to Hesiod, because of a trick by which Prometheus secured for man the choicest parts of meat in sacrifices to the gods. Prometheus' punishment was to be nailed to a mountain peak in the Caucasus range, while an eagle fed upon his liver. After ages of suffering, spent partly in the depths of Tartarus, Prometheus was set free by Heracles. In Aeschylus' version of the story, Prometheus knew a secret vital to the well-being of Zeus, that if Zeus should marry Thetis a son born of the union would dethrone him. In the two lost plays of the trilogy of which *Prometheus Bound* was a part the release of Prometheus and the revelation of the secret were the premises of a compromise, and the final solution made Zeus in some way incorporate into his own godhead the wisdom and philanthropy of Prome-theus. In Shelley's equally famous version, *Prometheus Unbound*, no com-promise is deemed possible, and Jupiter is overthrown.

Sometimes the story of **Pandora** is brought into connection with Prome-theus and his brother Epimetheus, the "Afterthinker."

In antiquity, Hesiod's *Works and Days* and *Theogony* and Aeschylus' *Prometheus Bound* are the principal literary treatments of the story of Prometheus. In the nineteenth century the story had a great vogue. In addi-tion to Shelley's *Prometheus Unbound* (1814), which is certainly one of the great poems of the century, there are, among many others, Byron's *Prome-theus* (1816) and Robert Bridges' "mask," *Prometheus the Fire-Giver* (1883).

Proserpina (pro-sur'pin-a), or **Proserpine** (pros'ur-pin), is Persephone, daugh-ter of Demeter and wife of **Hades.**

Protesilaus (prō-te-si-lā'us), a Greek, was the first warrior killed at Troy in the Trojan War. His death was destined to ensure victory for the Greeks. He had left at home a new bride, Laodamia. Her grief was so moving that the gods permitted Protesilaus to return briefly to the world, and when he died again, Laodamia died with him.

Proteus (prō'tūs) was a **Sea Deity.**

*read: Gaea), and is usually himself referred to as a Titan.

Psyche (sī'kē) was the bride of **Eros.**

Pygmalion (pig-mā'li-on) of Cyprus was a sculptor and a misogynist, or at least was quite dissatisfied with all the women of Cyprus and remained a bachelor. At last he created his own wife. He sculptured a marble woman so beautiful that he prayed to Aphrodite that he might find a wife as lovely as his statue; Aphrodite did better than he asked, for she brought the statue itself to life, and Pygmalion married it. Some modern writers have called the statue-wife Galatea. Child of this union was a girl, Paphos, eponym of the Cyprian city Paphos. Pygmalion has had a long and varied literary career, beginning with Ovid's *Metamorphoses*, 10, and extending to George Bernard Shaw's play, *Pygmalion,* which has recently become the musical comedy *My Fair Lady.* In between there have been John Marston's *The Metamorphosis of Pygmalion's Image* (1598), Thomas L. Beddoes' *Pygmalion* (1825), and W. S. Gilbert's *Pygmalion and Galatea* (1871).

The **Pygmies** were encountered by **Heracles** (*Minor stories*).

Pylades (pī'la-dēz) was the companion of Orestes. See **Atreus.**

Pylos (pī'los) was the home of Nestor of the **Trojan War.** Nestor is called Pylian.

Pyramus (pir'a-mus) and **Thisbe** lived in Babylon, in adjoining houses with a common wall. Pyramus was a handsome youth, Thisbe a beautiful girl. They were very much in love, but their families would not permit them to marry or even to meet openly. There was a small chink in the common wall of their houses, and through this the lovers used to exchange vows and endearments. But the chink was very small, and the lovers were unsatisfied. They determined to elope, and arranged to meet by night at the tomb of Ninus, just outside the city. Thisbe arrived first, and as she did she saw a lion, its jaws bloodstained from a recent meal of animal flesh, going to a nearby spring for a drink. Thisbe hid in terror, and in her fright dropped her veil. When the lion returned from the spring it saw the veil and picked it up. At this point Pyramus arrived, saw the veil in the bloody jaws of the lion, supposed that Thisbe had been devoured, and ran his sword through his body. As he lay dying, Thisbe came back, saw the sword and the veil, realized what had happened, and joined Pyramus in death by plunging the same sword into her breast. Ovid tells the story in the *Metamorphoses*, 4; Chaucer, in *The Legend of Good Women*; and Shakespeare uses it (humorously) in *A Midsummer-Night's Dream.*

Pyrrha (pir'a) was the wife of **Deucalion.**

Pyrrhus (pir'us) is another name of Neoptolemus, son of Achilles. See **Trojan War** (*The fall*).

Pythia (pith′i-a) is what **Apollo's** priestess at Delphi was called.

Pythian (pith′i-an) is an epithet of Apollo.

Python (pī′thon) was a serpent killed by **Apollo** when he took over the oracle at Delphi.

Quirinus (kwi-rī′nus) is the name of the deified **Romulus.**

Remus (rē′mus) was the twin brother of **Romulus.**

Rhadamanthus (rad-a-man′thus), or **Rhadamanthys,** of Crete became a judge of the underworld. See **Hades.**

Rhea (rē′a) was the wife of **Cronus.**

R(h)ea Silvia (rē′a sil′vi-a) was the mother of **Romulus** and Remus.

Rhesus (rē′sus), a Thracian prince, was an ally of the Trojans in the **Trojan War** (*Iliad*).

Ripheus (rif′ūs), a minor figure in the story of Aeneas, was made a symbol of justice by Dante. *

Romulus (rom′ū-lus) was the founder of Rome, thus sharing with Aeneas, founder of the Roman people, the honor of being the father of the Romans. When Aeneas died, he was succeeded as ruler of Lavinium by his son Ascanius, who in his turn founded and ruled over Alba Longa. Ascanius was succeeded at Alba Longa by Silvius, who was either the son of Aeneas and Lavinia or the son of Ascanius. Silvius was followed by an unbroken succession of descendants, the rule being handed down from father to son for some three centuries, when we come to the brothers Numitor and Amulius. Amulius, the younger, drove out the rightful king, Numitor, and usurped the throne; he forced R(h)ea Silvia, Numitor's daughter, to become a Vestal Virgin, so that she could have no descendants to claim the throne. But Mars fell in love with Rea Silvia and made her pregnant with twins. When they were born, Rea Silvia was put to death, and the twins, who were Romulus and Remus, were set adrift in the Tiber, in a basket. They were found by the edge of the river, at a point which was later in the very heart of the city of Rome, by a she-wolf, who nursed them. Then a shepherd named Faustulus took them home, and he and his wife, Acca Larentia, brought the children up.

    Years later Remus, now a youth, was captured by the shepherds of Numi-

*read: Dante in the *Divine Comedy* (Paradiso 20.68).

tor while the brothers and a group of followers were raiding the herds of Alba Longa. A recognition followed between grandfather and grandsons. They formed a plot against the usurper Amulius, killed him, and restored Numitor to power. Romulus and Remus decided to found a new city, and chose the site that was to become Rome. By augury it was decided that Romulus should be the official founder, and so the city was named for him. Shortly afterward, when the new city was still just in its beginnings, Remus leaped over the low wall that Romulus had built around his nascent city. Romulus was angry at this implied contempt for his city, and a fight ensued, in the course of which Remus was killed, some say by Romulus' own hand.

The new city was built, but the inhabitants were a band of youths, and they had no wives. To remedy this situation, they invited the neighboring communities to watch a show of some sort (apparently athletic contests), and while the audience was absorbed they seized the women and drove off the men, who had come unarmed. The neighbors, especially the Sabines, who had chiefly been plundered, came back under their king, Titus Tatius, and captured the Capitoline Hill. In this they were helped by the maiden Tarpeia, who betrayed the stronghold to them on terms that the warriors should give her what they wore on their left arms. Tarpeia had in mind their gold bracelets, but instead they piled upon her their shields and she was crushed to death. After fierce fighting in the Forum, between the Roman stronghold on the Palatine and the Sabine on the Capitoline, peace was made by the intercession of the women, and the Romans and Sabines became one people. Romulus soon after disappeared from earth mysteriously, and was worshiped as a god, under the name of Quirinus.

Some of the best stories of early Rome are rendered in ballad form in Macaulay's *Lays of Ancient Rome* (1842).

Salmacis (sal′ma-sis) was a nymph who loved Hermaphroditus. See **Hermes.**

Salmoneus (sal-mō′nūs), son of Aeolus, has two roles in mythology, as father of Tyro, and as the monarch who would be the rival of Zeus. He had his subjects call him Zeus, and imitated the thunderbolts of Zeus by driving his chariot over a brazen bridge. Zeus soon grew tired of the comedy and dispatched Salmoneus to Tartarus by hurling at him a real thunderbolt. Salmoneus' daughter, Tyro, was beloved of Poseidon, and by him was made pregnant
* with twins. Tyro's stepmother, Sidero (the "Iron One"), jealousy induced Salmoneus to punish his daughter cruelly for her love affair, which Sidero refused to believe had been with a deity. Tyro was therefore imprisoned by Salmoneus. Meanwhile, she had exposed her twins, Neleus and Pelias, at birth. After being suckled by a mare and a bitch, they were rescued and brought up by shepherds. Having grown to maturity, they found out their parentage, rescued Tyro from captivity, and put to death the cruel Sidero.

Neleus, father of Nestor of the Trojan War, and victim of an attack by **Heracles** (*Minor stories*), had a daughter, Pero. She was betrothed to Bias,

*read: jealously

a Thessalian prince. As bridal price, Neleus demanded of Bias the cattle of a certain Iphiclus, which were so valuable that Iphiclus would not part with them. Bias was aided in his dilemma by his brother Melampus, the greatest of all Greek prophets next to Theban Tiresias. Melampus could understand the language of all creatures, having gained this faculty as a reward for kindness. He had found a pair of snakes dead, with their young snakes alive beside them. He buried the parents and protected the young, and in gratitude they licked his ears, thus opening them to the speech of all animals and birds. In attempting to steal the cattle for his brother, Melampus was caught and imprisoned. While incarcerated, he overheard some worms who were gnawing at the beams of the building in which he was held saying that they had not far to gnaw, and that the building would presently fall. Melampus conveyed the message to his guard, who prudently and obligingly removed himself and his prisoner from the building. When the building at once fell, Iphiclus was impressed, and offered Melampus his freedom and the cattle if he could put an end to his unhappy state of childlessness. Melampus was able to oblige, having learned the answer to the problem from a vulture. Thus Melampus got the cattle, and Bias got Pero as wife.

Pelias, the twin brother of Neleus, appears in the story of the **Argonauts** and in that of Alcestis, who was his daughter. He had also a son, named Acastus. At one point Peleus came to Acastus for refuge and purification, having accidentally killed a man (Eurytion, in the Calydonian Boar Hunt). Acastus' wife, Hippolyte (or Astydamia or Cretheis), fell in love with Peleus, and when she was unable to seduce him, denounced him to Acastus, alleging that he had tried to seduce her. Acastus, unwilling to kill his guest outright, stole his sword from him during a hunting expedition on the mountains, while Peleus was asleep. When he woke, he found himself surrounded and threatened by the centaurs, until Chiron, the wise and humane centaur, rescued him and restored his sword to him. In some versions, Peleus later killed both Acastus and his wife in revenge.

Sarpedon (sar-pē'don), was (1) a son of Zeus and Europa of Crete; (2) a later son of Zeus, killed by Patroclus in the **Trojan War** (*Iliad*).

Saturn (sa'turn) is the Roman name of **Cronus.**

The **Satyrs** (sā'turz) were followers of **Dionysus,** and playmates of **Pan.**

The **Scaean** (sē'an) **Gate** was one of the gates of Troy.

Scylla (sil'a) was (1) a nymph transformed into a sea monster (see **Sea Deities** and **Odysseus,** *Sea adventures*); (2) daughter of Nisus of Megara (see **Athens**).

Sea Deities. Oceanus, the Titan, is little more than a geographical entity, the ocean stream which flows around the disk of the earth. He and his sister

Tethys are parents of three thousand daughters, called the Oceanids. Scarcely more of a person is Pontus, the Sea, son of Earth, but his descendants are of great interest. Nereus, the kindly Old Man of the Sea and a forerunner of Poseidon, is his son. Nereus is, by the Oceanid Doris, father of the fifty Nereids, the sea nymphs, among whom are Thetis, wife of Peleus and mother of Achilles (see **Trojan War**), and Galatea, with whom the Cyclops Polyphemus(see also under **Odysseus**, *Sea adventures*) fell in love. The shaggy and monstrous Cyclops tried to make himself more attractive, combing his hair and primping before a mirror, and sang to the nymph, but all in vain. Galatea loved the handsome youth Acis. One day Polyphemus came upon the lovers in each other's arms; Acis fled, but was crushed by a piece of a mountain flung at him by the Cyclops. The blood gushing from the dying youth was transformed by Galatea into a spring of water, which still flows from the rock that buried him. A third daughter of Nereus was Arethusa, who fled from the embrace of the Arcadian river god Alpheus. Arethusa swam all the way to Sicily and became the nymph of a spring on the island of Ortygia, part of Syracuse. Alpheus was said to have pursued her there, his river stream flowing beneath the surface of the sea.

Mating with his mother Earth, Pontus begot a race of monsters. Their children were Thaumas, Phorcys, Ceto, and Eurybia, whose names betoken monstrosities but who are little more than names. With their offspring we come to more familiar figures. Thaumas and the Oceanid Electra had as children Iris, the rainbow, who shares with Hermes the role of messenger of the gods, and the Harpies, three foul, food-snatching bird-women (see **Argonauts**, *Outward voyage*, and **Aeneas,** *Wanderings*). Phorcys and Ceto produced the Graeae and the Gorgons, for whom see under **Perseus,** and the serpent Ladon, who guards the golden apples in the garden of the Hesperides (see **Heracles,** eleventh Labor). The Gorgon Medusa mated with Poseidon to produce a sword-bearing man, Chrysaor, and a winged horse, Pegasus (see **Bellerophon**), who sprang from the trunk of Medusa when she was beheaded by Perseus. Chrysaor and the Oceanid Callirrhoe had as offspring the three-bodied Geryon (see **Heracles,** tenth Labor) and Echidna, whom Hesiod describes as "half a glancing-eyed nymph, fair of cheek, half a monstrous serpent, terrible and great, speckled, devouring raw meat." Echidna found her mate in the equally terrifying Typhoeus (see under **Zeus**), and their children were most of the animals of myth: Orth(r)us, dog of Geryon; Cerberus, the multiple-headed dog of the underworld (see **Hades**); the hundred-headed Hydra of Lerna, killed by **Heracles** (second Labor); and the Chimaera, who was part lion, part goat, and part snake, and was killed by **Bellerophon.** Orthus and his mother Echidna mated and produced the Sphinx of **Thebes** (*Oedipus*), and the Nemean lion which **Heracles** (first Labor) slew.

Probably these monstrous creatures, who are the main freaks of Greek
* myth, owe something to oriental influence. But it is no accident that they are the offspring of sea creatures. We find the same association with violence and monstrosity in **Poseidon,** who is the chief sea deity. Among other

*read: owe something to near Eastern influence.

minor sea deities we may mention Proteus, sometimes a son of Poseidon, but usually regarded as an older sea god. He is a shape-shifter and a prophet. To learn the future, you must catch him and hold him while he changes into many forms; when he resumes his own shape he will answer questions about things to come. Glaucus (also sometimes son of Poseidon) was a fisherman who was transformed into a sea god of merman shape when he ate a magic herb. He loved the beautiful sea nymph Scylla, but Scylla shunned him. Glaucus sought aid from the enchantress Circe, but Circe fell in love with him and, to be rid of a rival, threw into Scylla's bathing place herbs that transformed her, from the waist down, into a horrible monster ringed with barking dogs' heads. **Odysseus** (*Sea adventures*) encountered her in this form. Leucothea, who helps mariners in distress, and helped **Odysseus** (*Sea adventures*) on one occasion, was formerly the Theban princess Ino, wife of **Athamas;** Athamas went mad, killed his elder son, Learchus, and, thinking that they were animals that he was hunting, chased Ino and their younger son, Melicertes. Ino leaped into the sea with Melicertes in her arms, and both were transformed into the sea deities Leucothea and Palaemon.

Ovid, in the *Metamorphoses,* has the story of Arethusa (Book 5) and Galatea (Book 13). Shelley has a poem called *Arethusa* (1820).

Selene (se-lē'nē) is the moon goddess. See **Sky Deities.**

Semele (sem'e-le) was the mother of **Dionysus.**

The **Seven against Thebes.** See **Thebes.**

The **Sibyl** (sib'il) was a prophetess. See **Apollo.** She guided Aeneas to the underworld.

Sichaeus (sī-kē'us) was the husband of Dido, for whom see **Aeneas** (*Wanderings*).

Silenus (sī-lē'nus) is sometimes said to have been the nurse of **Dionysus.** The **Sileni** were followers of **Dionysus.**

Silvanus (sil-vā'nus), or **Sylvanus,** a Roman woodland deity, was often identified with **Pan.**

The **Silver Age** was the second of the **Ages of Man.**

Sinon (sī'non) was the Greek who persuaded the Trojans to accept the Wooden Horse. See **Trojan War** (*The fall*).

The **Sirens** were bird-women or mermaids who lured sailors to destruction by the enchantment of their song. They were named Parthenope, Ligea, and

Leucosia. See **Odysseus** (*Sea adventures;* in this story there are two sirens) and **Argonauts** (*Return voyage*).

Sirius (sir'i-us), the Dog Star, was the hound of Orion. See **Sky Deities.**

Sisyphus (sis'i-fus), founder of Corinth, was punished in the underworld. See **Hades.**

Sky Deities. First of all sky deities is Uranus, Father Sky himself, for whom see **Earth and Sky.** Zeus, too, is a sky god, as well as very many other things. Among the Titans, Phoebe and Hyperion are associated with the sky. Phoebe means "bright"; but she is only a name; by her brother Coeus she became mother of Leto, whose children, Artemis and Apollo, inherit their grandmother's name, Artemis often being called Phoebe, and Apollo Phoebus. In late ancient myth and in subsequent stories, Phoebus Apollo is the sun god, Artemis (Diana) or Phoebe the moon goddess; thus an English poet is likely to ascribe to them the adventures of the sun god and the moon goddess. Keats's Endymion is beloved of Diana; in Shakespeare Phaethon is son of Apollo. But originally there are separate deities: Helius (Sol) the sun god, Selene (Luna) the moon goddess, and also Eos (Aurora) the dawn goddess are children of the Titans Hyperion and Theia. Hyperion himself is perhaps the original sun god; Homer sometimes refers to the sun god as Helius Hyperion.

Helius drives his chariot across the sky each day, drawn by four horses, Pyroeis (fiery), Eoos (of the dawn), Aethon (blazing), and Phlegon (burning); by night he sails (presumably with his horses) in a golden cup on the stream of Oceanus back to the east. He is father of Aeetes, Medea's father (see **Argonauts,** *Colchis*), and of Circe (see **Odysseus,** *Sea adventures*). By the Oceanid Clymene, he is father of Phaethon (the "shining one"), who prevailed upon his father to let him drive his chariot across the sky one day. The famous and disastrous journey, in which the horses bolted and the chariot fell, ended in the death of Phaethon, when he tumbled to earth by the river Eridanus. His sisters, the Heliades, as they wept for him, were turned into poplar trees, and their tears became amber. Helius was the owner of a herd of cattle on the island of Thrinacia, by which the men of **Odysseus** (*Sea adventures,* end) came to grief. Clytia was loved and then deserted by the sun god; as she gazed longingly at him, she was transformed into a sunflower or heliotrope.

Selene is little other than simply the moon, except in the story of Endymion, the handsome young shepherd on Mount Latmus in Caria, with whom she fell in love. As he slept in a cave, she would come down from the sky night after night and caress him. Finally, when Zeus became aware of this affair, he punished Endymion (for it is the mortal who suffers), by sentencing him to everlasting sleep. He still sleeps in his cave on Latmus, and Selene still absents herself from the sky to visit him.

Eos is sometimes a charioteer, with two steeds. Especially, however, she is the lover and seizer of handsome youths. Tithonus was one mortal youth whom she carried off. She prevailed upon Zeus to grant him immortality, but she forgot to ask eternal youth for him, and so Tithonus shriveled away to nothingness, until only his voice was left. Their son was the Ethiopian prince Memnon, slain by Achilles in the **Trojan War** (*Late events*). The giant hunter Orion is said to have been carried off by Eos at one point; but his better-known adventures concern **Artemis** and the Pleiades, for whom see just below. The Athenian prince Cephalus (for whose story otherwise see **Athens**) was another youth loved and seized by Eos.

From late antiquity there have come innumerable stories of how persons of mythology were transformed into stars or constellations. Quite generally, these accounts are only minor appendages to other stories, as in the tales of Andromeda, Cepheus, and Cassiopeia, for whom see **Perseus,** and Callisto, for whom see **Artemis.** There are two groups, the Pleiades and the Hyades, who are principally conspicuous as constellations. The Pleiades, daughters of Atlas, son of the Titan Iapetus and the Oceanid Pleione, are seven nymphs only one of whom, Maia, mother of **Hermes** by Zeus, is well known other than as a part of the constellation. The Hyades are said to have been the nymphs of Nysa who nursed Dionysus, and whom Zeus changed into stars. Orion the hunter is another prominent star figure, who is said to pursue as suitor the Pleiades, who ever elude him. His dog, Sirius the Dog Star, accompanies him. Endymion has been much favored by poets, and Keats's *Endymion* (1818) stands conspicuous among poems about him. For an account of Keats's poem and others in English, see Edward S. Le Comte, *Endymion in England* (1944). The story of Phaethon is told well and at length by Ovid in the *Metamorphoses*, 1. See also Tennyson, *Tithonus* (1860), and George Meredith, *Phaethon* (1867).

Sol (sol) is the sun god. See **Sky Deities.**

The **Sphinx** was a bird-woman who harassed **Thebes** (*Oedipus*) until vanquished.

The **Stymphalian** (stim-fā′li-an) **Birds** were overcome by **Heracles** (fifth Labor).

Styx (stiks), one of the rivers of the underworld (see **Hades**), is called by Hesiod the chief daughter of the Titans Oceanus and Tethys. To Pallas, son of the Titans Crius and Eurybia, Styx bore Emulation, Victory (Nike), and Zeus's helpers, Strength and Force. Styx is noted for two things: she and her children helped **Zeus** in his battle against the Titans, and it is by her name that the gods swear their most solemn and inviolable oaths.

Sylvanus (sil-vā′nus) is **Silvanus.**

The **Symplegades** (sim-pleg′a-dēz) were the clashing rocks passed by the **Argonauts** (*Outward voyage*).

Syrinx (sir'inks) was a nymph whom **Pan** loved.

Talos (tā'los) was a mechanical giant who guarded Crete. See **Argonauts** (*Return voyage*).

Tantalus (tan'ta-lus) was the father of **Pelops** and a famous victim in the underworld. See **Hades.**

Tarpeia (tar-pē'a) was a girl who betrayed the Capitol to the Sabines. See **Romulus.**

Tartarus (tar'ta-rus) is the lowest region of the underworld, and the place of punishment. See **Hades.**

Taurians (taw'ri-anz) were Thracians in whose country Iphigenia was a priestess. See **Atreus.**

Telamon (tel'a-mon), son of **Aeacus,** took part in several heroic enterprises and was father of Ajax.

Telegonus (te-leg'o-nus) was (in some post-Homeric stories) the son of **Odysseus** (*Ithaca*) and Circe.

Telemachus (te-lem'a-kus) was the son of **Odysseus** (*Ithaca*) and Penelope.

Telephus (tel'e-fus), son of **Heracles** (*Minor stories*), was accidentally attacked by the Greeks at the beginning of the **Trojan War** (*Rallying of the host*).

Tellus (tel'us) is the Roman name for Mother Earth (see **Earth and Sky**).

Tempe (tem'pē) is a famous valley in Thessaly.

Tereus (tēr'ūs) was the husband of Procne. See **Athens.**

Terpsichore (turp-sik'o-rē) is one of the nine **Muses,** patroness of dancing.

Tethys (tē'this) was a minor **Sea Deity** and a **Titan.**

Teucer (tū'ser) was (1) a Greek hero of the Trojan War; (2) an early Trojan prince, from whom the Trojans are sometimes called Teucrians.

Thalia (tha-li'a) was (1) one of the nine **Muses,** patroness of comedy; (2) one of the three **Charites** (Graces).

Thamyris (tham'i-ris) was a minstrel who was punished by the **Muses.**

Thaumas (thaw′mas) was a minor **Sea Deity.**

Thebes (thēbz), in Boeotia, is the site of some of the most famous of all Greek myths. In addition to the stories of Dionysus and Heracles, which have close connections with Thebes, there are the following main parts to the Theban legend: the career of its founder, Cadmus; the story of Dirce and Antiope and her sons, and that of Niobe the proud; the tragedy of Oedipus and the story of his daughter Antigone; the expedition of the Seven against Thebes and the consequent stories of the Epigoni and of Alcmaeon. All these stories are of sufficient length and fame to merit separate treatment, but since the connections among them are intimate and numerous, it is convenient to treat them all here as parts of the legend of Thebes.

Cadmus. Cadmus was sent by his father, Agenor of Tyre, in search of his sister, Europa. On consulting the Delphic oracle, Cadmus was told to abandon the search, and to found a city where a cow which he was to follow should lie down to rest. Cadmus duly came to the site of what was to be Thebes. Then he and his men went to draw water from a nearby fountain, and there encountered a dragon, son of Ares. Cadmus killed the dragon, and then, at Athena's command, sowed the teeth of the dragon. Armed men sprang up, who, when Cadmus threw a stone among them, fell to such furious strife that presently only five weary survivors remained. (Compare the similar incident in the story of the **Argonauts,** *Colchis*). These, called the Sparti (the "sown men"), were the ancestors of great Theban families.

Cadmus married Harmonia, daughter of Ares and Aphrodite. The wedding feast was a great affair, with all the gods attending and bringing gifts, including a robe and necklace made by Hephaestus, which reappear several times in the stories of Thebes. The children of this union were a son, Polydorus, who succeeded to the throne, and several daughters, of whom Semele, Agave, and Ino appear in the story of **Dionysus;** for Ino, see also under **Sea Deities.** Son of Agave and Echion (one of the Sparti) was Pentheus, for whom see **Dionysus.** Later Cadmus and Harmonia left Thebes; Cadmus became king of the Illyrians, and he and Harmonia were eventually turned into snakes and sent by Zeus to the Elysian Fields.

Antiope and Dirce. Polydorus and his son Labdacus reigned without incident. At Labdacus' death Lycus became ruler. His niece, Antiope, was beloved of Zeus, and by him became pregnant with twins. To escape her family's anger (for they did not believe her lover to be divine) Antiope ran away to Sicyon, but was pursued by Lycus and dragged back to Thebes. On the way, twin boys were born and exposed, but were saved and reared by a shepherd. Antiope, cruelly treated by Lycus and by his wife, Dirce, eventually escaped and took refuge with the very shepherd who had saved her sons. The boys, now grown to manhood, were Amphion, a great musician, and Zethus, a great warrior. A recognition was effected between mother and sons, and the sons proceeded to take revenge on their mother's tormentors. They put Lycus to the sword, and their vengeance on Dirce is famous: they bound her to the horns of a bull, which dragged her to death. Amphion and Zethus became rulers of Thebes, Amphion providing a wall for the city by charming the stones into place by the magic of his lyre-playing. Zethus married Thebe, from whom the city was named, but who is otherwise unknown; Amphion married Niobe, daughter of Tantalus.

Niobe. Niobe's famous story can be told briefly. She had seven sons and seven daughters and was inordinately proud of them, even boasting that she was superior in respect of children to Leto, mother of Apollo and Artemis. Leto did not endure for long Niobe's foolish boasts. She sent her two children to inflict a swift and terrible punishment on the mortal mother. All the sons of Niobe fell before the arrows of Apollo, all the daughters before those of Artemis. Niobe's grief was as limitless as her pride had been. Finally she left Thebes and went back to her father's home in Lydia. There she was turned to stone, and became Mount Sipylus, from which streams of water flow forever, the tears of Niobe.

Oedipus. Laius was the next king of Thebes. To him it was prophesied that if a son was born to him the son was destined to kill him and marry his wife, Jocasta. Laius disregarded the warning, and a son was born. The child was exposed on Mount Cithaeron, but a herdsman from Corinth rescued him and took him to the childless King Polybus of Corinth, who reared him as his own, not knowing whence he came. The child, given the name Oedipus, reached maturity at Corinth. When a companion taunted him with not being the son of Polybus, Oedipus went to Delphi to ask the oracle about his parentage. No direct answer was given, but Oedipus was told that he would kill his father and commit incest with his mother. At once resolving never to go back to Corinth, he struck off in the direction of Thebes, heading for home, though he did not know it. At a meeting place of three roads he encountered a group, consisting of an old man in a mule cart and a few attendants, coming toward Delphi. When this group, asserting their right of way, tried to force Oedipus from the path, Oedipus lost his temper and killed all of them but one. Oedipus went on to Thebes, where he found the city harassed by the Sphinx, a monstrous winged creature with a woman's face and a lion's body, which asked all passers-by a riddle and killed all who could not answer it. Oedipus answered the riddle, and the Sphinx fell dead. The grateful Thebans made him king and gave him the widowed Jocasta as his wife. For King Laius had disappeared. It was he that Oedipus had killed on the road. Oedipus and Jocasta had four children, two boys, Eteocles and Polynices, and two girls, Antigone and Ismene. After Oedipus had ruled for years in Thebes, the city was overwhelmed by a blight. The oracle at Delphi announced that the city could be made wholesome only if Laius's murderer were driven out. Gradually the whole terrible truth came out, in part through Oedipus' own efforts, in part through the seer Tiresias, in part through the one man who had escaped at the crossroads. Oedipus, in an agony of remorse and despair, blinded himself. Jocasta took her own life. The later history of Oedipus is variously told. In some versions he stays in Thebes; in others he is exiled and finally ends his life just outside Athens, where a mysterious voice from heaven calls to him and he disappears from the sight of men on a rocky hillside of Colonus.

Seven against Thebes. Creon became regent of Thebes after the fall of Oedipus, until the sons were old enough to rule. When they grew to maturity, they brought further disaster to Thebes, for they were doomed to destruction by each other's hand, having been cursed by their father. The circumstances of the curse are variously told; probably originally it was simply a matter of the sons' inheriting the incurable taint which Oedipus had acquired by his involuntary sins. The two brothers agreed to alternate the rule, in periods of one year. Eteocles had first turn, and at the end of his year declined to yield. Meanwhile Polynices had gone to Argos, where he had married the daughter of King Adrastus. When Eteocles refused to give up the throne, Polynices appealed to his father-in-law, who, having consented to help him, organized the expedition known as the Seven against Thebes.

The seven leaders were Adrastus; Polynices; Tydeus, who was another son-in-law of Adrastus and father of Diomedes of the Trojan War; Capaneus; Hippomedon; Parthenopaeus, the son of Milanion and **Atalanta;** and Amphiaraus, a famous prophet and descendant of Melampus (for whom see under **Salmoneus**). By his prophetic knowledge Amphiaraus knew that the expedition was doomed to failure and that he was certain to die; hence he was loath to go. But his wife, Eriphyle, sister of Adrastus, was bribed by Polynices, who gave her the famous necklace of Harmonia. On an earlier occasion Adrastus and Amphiaraus had agreed that any dispute between them should be settled by Eriphyle, who now insisted that her husband join the attack. He did so, but as he left he made his two young sons swear to take vengeance on their mother for sending him to his death.

Only the most familiar of the numerous incidents of the expedition can be mentioned here. First is an incident that occurred on the march, at Nemea, where Opheltes, the infant son of King Lycurgus of Nemea, was left unattended by his nurse Hypsipyle (the exiled queen of Lemnos; for her earlier history see under **Argonauts,** *Outward voyage*) while she led the soldiers to a spring. A dragon seized and killed the child and was in its turn killed by the Seven. Opheltes was renamed by the gloomy Amphiaraus and called Archemorus (the "beginner of doom"). The child's funeral was celebrated with athletic contests, and this was the origin of the Nemean Games. Before the Seven reached Thebes, Tydeus was sent ahead on an embassy, to demand Polynices' rights. The mission was fruitless, and on the way back Tydeus was ambushed by fifty Theban warriors. He killed all but one whom he spared to take the news to Thebes. The Seven now reached Thebes, but before battle was joined, Menoeceus, son of Creon, flung himself from the wall as a sacrifice, the prophet Tiresias having declared that Menoeceus' death would ensure victory for Thebes.

Each of the Seven attacked one of the seven gates of Thebes, and met in combat a defending champion. All the invaders except Adrastus died. Capaneus was the first to die; rushing upon the walls and shouting that not even Zeus could stop him, he was blasted at once by a thunderbolt. Tydeus was mortally wounded in a duel with Melanippus of Thebes, who was killed in the same duel. The head of Melanippus was brought to Tydeus, who in his fury split it open and devoured the brains. Athena had been approaching to heal Tydeus' wounds and bestow immortality upon him, but, repelled by such barbaric conduct, she retired in disgust and left him to die. As Amphiaraus turned to flee in his chariot, Zeus caused the ground to open up and swallow him, horses, chariot, and all. Adrastus escaped on his immortal talking steed Arion. Eteocles and Polynices met in combat and died by each other's hand, fulfilling Oedipus' curse.

Antigone. Creon now became king of Thebes. His first edict was an interdiction of burial for the corpse of the traitor Polynices. Antigone, Oedipus' daughter, refused to obey the edict, though her sister Ismene urged obedience. Antigone, caught attempting to bury Polynices, was entombed in a cave to starve to death. Before this death could ensue she took her own life; when Haemon, Creon's son and Antigone's fiancé, found her dead, he took his life. Finally, Eurydice, wife of Creon, hanged herself when she heard of Haemon's death. Another story has it that Creon refused burial to all the fallen attackers. Thereupon Adrastus and a crowd of Argive women petitioned Theseus of Athens to force Thebes to permit decent burial. By force of arms, Theseus compelled the Thebans to do so.

Epigoni. The expedition of the Epigoni against Thebes, though much less celebrated, was more successful. The Epigoni were the sons of the Seven: Alcmaeon and Amphilochus, sons of Amphiaraus; Diomedes, son of Tydeus; Sthenelus, son of Capaneus; Promachus, son of Parthenopaeus; Euryalus, son of Mecisteus (brother of Adrastus, and sometimes among the Seven); Aegialeus, son of Adrastus; and Thersander, son of Polynices. Some of the events are mere variations on the story of the Seven: Eriphyle is bribed by Thersander with the robe of Harmonia to persuade her sons to join; only Aegialeus is killed. The Thebans were beaten, and Thersander was made king. Adrastus died of grief for his son's death.

The story of Alcmaeon, though not a Theban story, follows naturally here. Alcmaeon was obedient to his father, Amphiaraus, and killed his mother, Eriphyle. As a result he was pursued, like Orestes (see under **Atreus**), by the Furies. His subsequent wanderings and adventures were numerous and obscure. The fatal necklace and robe were finally dedicated to Apollo at Delphi, and remained in the god's shrine there.

Among Theban figures, Oedipus and his family, and among incidents, the attack of the Seven, have attracted most literary interest. Sophocles' three plays, *Oedipus Tyrannus, Oedipus at Colonus,* and *Antigone,* have inspired numerous imitations or rival efforts, among them Oedipus plays by Seneca, Pierre Corneille (1659), Dryden and Lee (1679), Voltaire (1718), Shelley (1819, a travesty of the theme, written as a political satire), and, in the present century, André Gide and Jean Cocteau. There have been *Antigones* by Alfieri (1777) and Jean Anouilh (1944). The story of the Seven is used in Aeschylus' play, *Seven against Thebes,* and is the subject of a long Latin epic by Statius. E. M. Forster's short story, *The Road from Colonus* in *The Collected Tales* (1947), and T. S. Eliot's play, *The Elder Statesman* (1958), both reflect Sophocles' *Oedipus at Colonus.* Also deserving of mention are Ovid's account of Niobe, in the *Metamorphoses,* 6, and Tennyson's *Tiresias* (1885).

Themis (thē'mis), a **Titan,** was a wife of **Zeus** (also of Iapetus), a **Mother-Goddess,** and the deity of the Delphic oracle before Apollo.

Thersites (thur-sī'tez) was the troublemaker among the Greeks in the Trojan War.

Theseus (thē'sūs) was the son of Aegeus, king of Athens. Being childless, Aegeus consulted the oracle of Apollo at Delphi. He was given an enigmatic reply which he could not interpret, and went to Troezen for advice from King Pittheus. Here he met and fell in love with Aethra, daughter of Pittheus. He left Aethra pregnant and returned to Athens, bidding her to rear the child that would be born, if it was a boy, and to send him to Athens when he was strong enough to roll away a great stone and take the sword and sandals which Aegeus left buried under it. In due time a son, Theseus, was born. (Sometimes it is said that the father of Theseus was Poseidon, and it may be that Aegeus, who is the eponym of the Aegean Sea, is simply a local form of Poseidon.) Theseus grew to young manhood, rolled away the stone, and set out for Athens, equipped with the sandals and the sword. Old Pittheus urged him to go by the shorter and safer sea voyage, but Theseus, eager for adventure, went by land, and on the way engaged in six formidable contests.

Early adventures. First he met Periphetes, son of Hephaestus, a robber who dispatched his victims with a great brazen club which he always carried. Theseus overcame him, and henceforth he carried Periphetes' brazen club. (The carrying of a club is only one of many details in which the career of Theseus resembles that of Heracles, and very likely was modeled upon it by Athenian storytellers.) Next came Sinis, called Pityocamptes (the "Pine Bender"), a robber who disposed of his victims by bending two pine trees toward each other, tying the subject's arms to one of them and his legs to the other, and then releasing the trees so that they sprang up, tearing the unfortunate man in half. Theseus killed Sinis by this method. The third encounter was with Phaea, a great wild sow of Crommyon, which was apparently causing much trouble. Theseus speared it, in a sort of private equivalent of the Calydonian Boar Hunt. Still another robber was Sciron of Megara. He used to force each passer-by to wash his feet at the edge of a sea cliff which is still called the Scironian Rocks; then he would kick the wretch over the cliff, to a great turtle waiting in the sea below to devour him. Theseus kicked Sciron off to his own turtle. At Eleusis Theseus overcame the skillful and cruel wrestler, Cercyon. Finally, nearing Athens, Theseus encountered Procrustes (sometimes called Damastes or Polypemon). Procrustes had his own kind of hospitality: he willingly entertained all passers-by but insisted that they fit exactly the bed on which he had them sleep. When they did not fit it exactly, he stretched or lopped off their limbs to make them fit. Theseus performed the same operation on Procrustes, who apparently did not fit his own bed.

Arrived at Athens, Theseus had trouble getting himself established with his father Aegeus, chiefly because Medea, whose earlier history is told under * **Argonauts,** was then Aegeus' wife, and did not wish Theseus to replace her influence over Aegeus. In an attempt to get rid of him, Medea sent him against the bull that **Heracles** (seventh Labor) had brought from Crete, and that now was ravaging the plain of Marathon. Theseus overcame the bull, and then Medea tried to poison him. But in the nick of time Aegeus recognized his son, by his sword and sandals, and accepted him. Medea retreated to Asia, where her son Medus became ancestor of the Medes.

Minotaur. A much stiffer ordeal now confronted Theseus. Some years before, Androgeus, son of Minos of Crete, had been killed in an athletic contest at Athens. Minos had consequently invaded Athens and forced the city to pay to Crete an annual tribute of seven youths and seven maidens, who were sent into the Labyrinth, a great structure with an infinitude of winding passages, such that once in, nobody could find his way out again. In the Labyrinth lurked a terrible creature, the Minotaur, half man and half bull, who each year would kill and devour the Athenian youths and maidens. (For Daedalus, builder of the Labyrinth, the birth of the Minotaur, and other related stories, see **Crete.**)

Theseus insisted on becoming one of the sacrificial youths, and the sorrowful voyage to Crete began. Old Aegeus tearfully took leave of his son and sent the ship away with black sails hoisted, enjoining upon Theseus to change the sails to white on the return voyage if he were successful and should indeed return. If Theseus should fail and die, the crew were to leave the black sails aloft. En route, Theseus gave an indication of the divine backing which he enjoyed, when he dove into the sea and recovered a ring cast into it by Minos; he was helped in this by Amphitrite. (Compare the tradition, mentioned above, that Theseus was son of Poseidon.)

When they reached Crete, the daughter of Minos, Ariadne, at once fell in love with Theseus and helped him achieve success. When he entered the Labyrinth, Theseus carried a ball of thread given him by Ariadne (to whom Hephaestus had given it) so that he could unwind the thread as he went and

*read: Aegeus's

by its guidance retrace his steps. Theseus found and slew the Minotaur and then led the Athenian captives to safety. They fled from Crete, and Ariadne went with them. But Theseus deserted Ariadne, "forgot" her, on the island of Naxos, where **Dionysus** later found her and made her his bride. As the ship approached the Attic coast, old Aegeus was standing at the brink of the south, seaward side of the Acropolis, scanning the horizon anxiously. In time he caught a glimpse of sails, and they were black. In despair, Aegeus threw himself onto the rocks below. Theseus, speeding merrily homeward, had forgotten again.

Later adventures. Theseus was now king of Athens. The usual picture of him in Athenian literature shows a sagacious and benign ruler, helping the worthy (befriending the aged Oedipus of Thebes, for example), championing the weak (supporting the suppliant Argive women; see **Thebes,** *Antigone*). Yet the specific mythological material concerning Theseus often suggests rather a continuation of the restless spirit of adventure characteristic of his youth. Like so many heroes, he had an encounter with the Amazons. Either he accompanied Heracles on his expedition against them or made his own, and abducted the Amazon Antiope, or Hippolyte, by whom he had a son, Hippolytus. The Amazons, in return, invaded Attica and were driven off only after a fierce struggle. With his friend Pirithous, the Thessalian prince of the Lapiths, Theseus had various adventures. At the wedding of Pirithous and Hippodamia, a great fight broke out between the Lapiths and the centaurs, who had too much wine at the wedding feast, and tried to rape the bride. Theseus fought doughtily in this celebrated affair. Another time Theseus and Pirithous kidnaped Helen, and her brothers, Castor and Polydeuces, came and took her back (this was before her marriage to Menelaus). Theseus and Pirithous even tried to kidnap Persephone from the underworld. This undertaking was a complete fiasco; both of them were caught and detained below, Pirithous forever, Theseus until Heracles, who had gone down to get Cerberus, released him.

Hippolytus. The story of Hippolytus and Phaedra belongs in our account of Theseus. While Theseus was away, Phaedra, wife of Theseus and sister of Ariadne, fell in love with her stepson Hippolytus. Hippolytus, who was a most virginal young man, devoted to hunting and the worship of Artemis, rejected Phaedra's advances in horror. Humiliated, Phaedra hanged herself, but for revenge she left a note saying that Hippolytus had violated her. Theseus returned, found the note, and banished Hippolytus from the kingdom, at the same time calling upon Poseidon to accomplish the young man's death. As Hippolytus sadly set forth for exile, driving his chariot along the shore, a great monster appeared from the sea and caused the horses to bolt. Hippolytus became involved in the wreckage of his chariot and was fatally injured. Before his son died, Theseus learned the truth and they were reconciled. Sometimes there is an epilogue to the story, in which Asclepius tries to restore Hippolytus to life (see **Apollo**).

Finally, Menestheus, a descendant of Erechtheus, banished Theseus from Athens and became king. Theseus went to the rocky island of Scyros, and lost his life there when King Lycomedes pushed him off a cliff.

Theseus himself does not figure largely in literature as a hero. Both Catullus (*Poem* 64) and Chaucer, in *The Legend of Good Women*, tell the story of Ariadne. The tragic love of Phaedra for Hippolytus has been treated often in plays, including Euripides' *Hippolytus*, Seneca's *Hippolytus*, Racine's *Phèdre* (1677), and Edmund Smith's *Phaedra and Hippolytus* (1707).

Thetis (thē′tis), a Nereid, was the mother of Achilles. See **Trojan War** (*Background*).

Thisbe (thiz′bē) was beloved of **Pyramus.**

Thoas (thō′as) was the king of the Taurians. See **Atreus.**

Thyestes (thī-es′tēz) was the brother of **Atreus.**

The **Thyrsus** (thir′sus) is the wand of **Dionysus** and his followers.

Tiresias (tī-rē′si-as) of Thebes, son of a nymph, Chariclo, and descended on the paternal side from one of the Sown Men of Thebes, was the greatest of all mythological prophets. He is important above all as a figure in many of the stories of **Thebes;** he is consulted also, in the underworld, by Odysseus. Tiresias lived as both man and woman. Born a man, he became a woman when, coming upon two snakes copulating, he killed the female. Seven years later he came upon another two snakes copulating, killed the male, and became a man again. Because of his broad experience he was called upon to settle a dispute between Zeus and Hera. They were arguing about which gained greater enjoyment from sexual intercourse, man or woman. When Tiresias ruled that a woman's enjoyment is far greater, Hera, who had taken the other side in the debate, was furious and struck Tiresias blind. Zeus granted him unerring prophetic skill. See Tennyson's *Tiresias* (1885); Tiresias is an important figure in Eliot's *The Waste Land* (1922).

Tisamenus (ti-sam′en-us) was the son of Orestes and Hermione. See **Atreus.**

Tisiphone (ti-sif′ō-nē) was one of the Furies. See **Hades** (end of article).

The **Titans** (tī′tanz) are the most important set of offspring of **Earth and Sky.** They are twelve in number, and most of them have, or seem to have, a connection with natural phenomena. Oceanus is the ocean stream surrounding the world, Tethys is also associated with water, Hyperion is a sun god, Themis and Rhea are connected with the power and fertility of the earth. The name of Phoebe means "bright," and she was later identified with the moon and with her own granddaughter, Artemis. Theia, "the divine," seems to be a sky figure. Coeus and Crius are vague figures, while Iapetus is known only as the father of Prometheus and Atlas. Mnemosyne, "Memory," bore the nine **Muses** to Zeus. **Cronus** is by far the most important of the Titans; for the story of how he replaced his father as ruler and for an account of his rule, see under his name. The story of the defeat of the Titans by Zeus and the younger gods is given under **Zeus.**

Ten of the Titans married one another. Coeus and Phoebe had two children, Leto (mother by Zeus of Apollo and Artemis) and Asteria (mother of Hecate). Cronus and Rhea, Oceanus and Tethys, Iapetus and Themis, and Hyperion and Theia produced offspring of some importance, and in the case of Cronus and Rhea, of supreme importance, in myth. For them, see under **Cronus, Sea Deities, Prometheus,** and **Sky Deities,** respectively. Rhea and Themis are further mentioned also under **Mother-Goddesses.** Crius married Eurybia, daughter of Pontus (Sea) and Earth, and had as offspring Pallas, husband of the river Styx, Perses, father of Hecate, and Astraeus, husband of Eos the dawn goddess.

In ancient literature the Titans are described chiefly in Hesiod's *Theogony.* Keats has dealt with the theme of the fallen Titans in *Hyperion* (1818–1819) and *The Fall of Hyperion* (1819).

Tithonus (ti-thō'nus) was carried off by Eos. See **Sky Deities.**

Tityus (tit'i-us) was a giant punished in Tartarus. See **Hades** (*Underworld*).

Triptolemus (trip-tol'e-mus) of Eleusis was taught by Demeter how to grow wheat.

Triton (tri'ton) was the son of **Poseidon** by Amphitrite.

Troilus (trō'i-lus), son of Priam, was the hero of a medieval romance based on the **Trojan War** (*Early events*).

The **Trojan** (trō'jan) **War** is the latest in time and the most familiar of all the great occasions of Greek mythology. The figures and stories concerned in it have provided material for poets, painters, playwrights, and sculptors from the time of Homer to the present moment. To give an account of the story straight through, beginning *ab ovo*, "from the egg," although (as Horace says) no proper procedure for a poet, will do well enough in a mythological summary. But since we have already told the story of the Egg (see **Leda**), we shall begin instead with the Apple, which must be introduced by some mention of Peleus and Thetis.

Background. Peleus, son of Aeacus, while on the cruise of the Argonauts saw the Nereid Thetis and fell in love with her. Zeus also loved Thetis, but being warned that she would bear a son mightier than his father, Zeus yielded to Peleus. After Peleus had caught his elusive bride (she had the power of changing shape, becoming a snake, a lion, fire, etc.), a sumptuous wedding feast was held. All the gods attended except Eris, goddess of strife, who inadvertently was not invited. For revenge, Eris tossed in through a window a golden apple inscribed "For the Fairest." Hera, Athena, and Aphrodite all claimed it. Zeus, called on to arbitrate, referred the case to Paris, son of King Priam of Troy. One fact must yet be added concerning the marriage of Peleus and Thetis: their child was Achilles, greatest of all the Greek warriors at the siege of Troy.

The royal family of Troy began with Dardanus, son of Zeus and Electra, daughter of Atlas. Dardanus' son was Erichthonius, who in turn begot Tros, from whom Troy was named. Tros had three sons, Ilus, Assaracus, and Ganymedes. Ganymedes was carried off by the eagle of Zeus to become the cupbearer of Zeus, who, in return, gave Tros an immortal team of horses (later sought by **Heracles,** ninth Labor). From Assaracus descended, in succession, Capys, Anchises, and **Aeneas.** Son of Ilus was Laomedon, whose son was Priam. Priam had fifty sons and fifty daughters, including Paris (who is also called Alexander), Hector, and Cassandra. Before Priam's wife, Hecuba, gave birth to Paris, she dreamt that she gave birth to a firebrand. Because the dream interpreters warned Priam that the child to be born would cause the destruction of Troy, Priam exposed the infant Paris at birth. Rescued by shepherds, Paris was brought up as a shepherd on Mount Ida, and lived there in contentment with the nymph Oenone. Later, after the Judgment, he was recognized as Priam's son and took up his princely status, forsaking Oenone. The Judgment of Paris was, of course, his decision among the three contesting goddesses. Hermes brought them to him on Mount Ida. Hera guaranteed him power if she were selected; Athena promised military success; Aphrodite offered him the most beautiful woman in the world as his wife. Paris awarded the apple to Aphrodite.

Rallying of the host. The most beautiful woman in the world was Helen, daughter of Zeus and Leda, and wife of King Menelaus of Sparta. So potent was Helen's beauty that all the great chieftains of Greece had been her suitors, and when she chose Menelaus, all the rest swore an oath to avenge any insult to her honor, should need arise. Paris arrived at Sparta and was entertained by Menelaus for nine days. Then Menelaus went away to Crete, and Paris abducted Helen, or, with Aphrodite's aid, persuaded her to go back to Troy with him. The Greek leaders rallied to the aid of Menelaus, under the leadership of Agamemnon, Menelaus' brother, king of Mycenae and over-lord of a large area of Greece. There are several stories concerning the rallying of the host. Odysseus, happily married in the far-off island of Ithaca, was loath to leave his faithful wife, Penelope, and their infant son, Telemachus. When envoys came to summon him, he feigned madness, and, yoking an ox and an ass, plowed a field and sowed it with salt. But one of the envoys was Palamedes, a match even for Odysseus in shrewdness. Palamedes set the baby Telemachus in the path of Odysseus' plow, and when the father swerved to avoid hitting the child his sanity was revealed and he was taken. Achilles, too, was in hiding, though not of his will. Thetis, who knew that participation in the coming war would be fatal to him, hid him away at the court of King Lycomedes of the island of Scyros, where Achilles was disguised in women's clothing. Odysseus went to the island disguised as a peddler of jewelry. With the jewels he placed some weapons of war; when Achilles instinctively reached for the weapons, he was revealed.

Finally the host was assembled. Among the principal heroes were Agamemnon; Menelaus; Achilles; Diomedes, son of Tydeus of the Seven against Thebes, and himself one of the Epigoni (see **Thebes**); Ajax, son of Telamon and cousin of Achilles; Nestor from Pylos; Idomeneus of Crete; Ajax the Locrian; Philoctetes, son of Poeas, friend of **Heracles** (*Deianira*); Machaon and Podalirius, sons of Asclepius and themselves great physicians; Patroclus, close companion of Achilles; and Teucer, half-brother of Ajax, son of Telamon. On the Trojan side, most of the prominent figures were the sons of Priam, especially Hector and Paris. Aeneas, whose own story is told elsewhere, is not very prominent in the Trojan War. He and Antenor were hostile to Paris and to the war. Leaders of the Lycian allies of Troy were Sarpedon, son of Zeus, and Glaucus, descendant of Bellerophon.

The first attempt to sail to Troy was a failure. The armada got off its course and landed in Teuthrania, land of King Telephus, son of Heracles. Thinking they were at Troy, the Greeks landed and opened battle, but soon, realizing their error, withdrew. Meanwhile Telephus had been wounded by Achilles; he was told by an oracle that only Achilles could heal the wound he had inflicted. Telephus followed the host back to Greece and prevailed on Achilles to heal him. In return, he guided the Greeks to Troy on their next attempt. The host now assembled, for the second voyage, at the port of Aulis. Here Agamemnon incurred the displeasure of Artemis by shooting a deer sacred to her. Adverse winds then kept the ships from sailing, and it was learned that only the sacrifice of Iphigenia, daughter of Agamemnon, could appease the goddess and bring a sailing wind. Iphigenia was summoned, on the pretext that she was to marry Achilles, and was put to death. Sometimes it is said that at the last moment Artemis substituted a fawn for the maiden, who was swept away miraculously to the land of the Taurians, in Thrace, there to become a priestess of Artemis. See further under **Atreus**.

The ships could now sail. On the voyage, during a stop for water at the island of Lemnos, Philoctetes was bitten by a snake and the wound was so terrible that he could not be taken back on board ship. He was left an exile on Lemnos for ten years, with only the magic bow and arrows of Heracles (inherited from Philoctetes' father, Poeas) to sustain him.

Early events. It was destined that the first man to land at Troy must die, but that his death would ensure victory for the Greeks. The young warrior **Protesilaus** leaped forth first to death beneath the spear of Hector.

The Greeks besieged Troy for ten years. The early events of the siege are on the whole less famous than those of the final year. At some point Achilles ambushed and killed Troilus, a young son of Priam. (The elaborate medieval love story of Troilus and Cressida, with Pandarus as go-between, arose after the period of ancient myth with which we are concerned. In Homer, and in all other regular ancient stories of Troy, Troilus dies as a mere boy, there is no Cressida, and Pandarus shoots an arrow that causes the breaking of a truce during the siege and shortly afterward is killed by Achilles.) Another victim of Achilles was Cycnus, son of Poseidon, who was transformed into a swan (Greek *kyknos*) at his death. Palamedes, the rival of Odysseus, was, through the machinations of Odysseus, falsely accused of treachery to the army and was put to death.

Iliad. After nine years of skirmishing and attacks on minor strongholds in the neighborhood of Troy come the most familiar events of the siege, those that are told in the *Iliad*. When Agamemnon took away Achilles' prize of war, the maiden Briseis, Achilles quarreled violently with the leader and retired in anger from the fighting. Thetis, his mother, prevailed on Zeus to give victory to the Trojans while Achilles was gone from the battlefield. During his absence numerous incidents took place. A duel between Menelaus and Paris, meant to decide the entire issue, was broken off when Aphrodite rescued Paris, who was on the verge of defeat, by lifting him bodily away from the field of battle. Diomedes, who was, next to Achilles, the most dashing and brilliant of the young Greek warriors, achieved many victories during Achilles' absence from the field, even wounding Aphrodite, with the aid of Athena. Hector, after a tender farewell to his lovely wife, Andromache, and his infant son, Astyanax, left the protection of the walls of Troy for the last time. A duel between Hector and Ajax was interrupted by darkness, after Ajax had a little the better of it. Before long, however, the Greeks, being hard pressed, sent as ambassadors to Achilles, to urge his return to battle, Ajax, Odysseus, and Phoenix, an aged warrior who was a close friend of Achilles. Achilles refused the honorable amends offered and stayed in his tent.

A night interlude heartened the Greeks somewhat, when Diomedes and Odysseus, on a scouting expedition, captured a Trojan spy, Dolon, and after learning from him much about the layout of the Trojan camp (for the Trojan warriors had moved out of the city in pursuit of the Greeks and were en-camped on the plain), they put him to death. Then, acting on his information, they went to the encampment of Rhesus, a Thracian prince who had just arrived as an ally of Troy. They killed Rhesus and many of his men and made off with his valuable horses. But soon the Trojans stormed ahead again, and, led by Hector, began to set fire to the ships. Then at last Achilles relented, to the extent of permitting Patroclus to go into battle wearing his armor. Patroclus killed Sarpedon, son of Zeus, and then was himself killed by Hector and Apollo. Hector stripped from him the armor of Achilles, which he then donned. Achilles, in deep sorrow, his anger now transferred to Hector, re-sumed battle, in a new suit of armor and a new shield made for him by

Hephaestus, at the request of Thetis. Achilles was now merciless and invincible. After killing many Trojans and driving the rest back to the city, he met Hector in single combat and killed him. For days he dragged about the plains of Troy the body of his dead enemy attached to his chariot wheels. Finally, when old Priam, guided by Hermes, came to his tent and begged to be permitted to ransom his son's body, Achilles relented and Hector was buried by the Trojans. At this point the *Iliad* ends.

Late events. Fresh reinforcements for Troy now arrived, including a band of Amazons, led by their queen, Penthesilea. After killing Machaon, she met death at the hands of Achilles. It is sometimes said that even as he killed the queen, Achilles fell in love with her, and that Thersites, always the harsh critic and abuser of the leaders, perceiving this, taunted Achilles with it so violently that Achilles finally killed him. Another new arrival was Memnon, prince of Ethiopia, son of Eos and Tithonus (see under **Sky Deities**). Under his spear fell Antilochus, son of the aged Nestor. In time, Memnon fell before Achilles. When the men met in battle, the two divine mothers, Thetis and Eos, each begged Zeus to grant victory to her son. Zeus weighed the warriors' souls in the balance (the event is called the Psychostasia), and the pan of the balance holding Memnon's soul sank, dooming him to defeat.

Soon after, Achilles met his death, struck by an arrow shot by Paris, whose aim was guided by Apollo. The story of how Thetis dipped the infant Achilles in the River Styx is not found in Homer or early myth, but has become a familiar detail. She held him by one heel, and that heel, unwetted by the Stygian water, alone was vulnerable; that is where Paris shot him. A contest followed concerning who should have Achilles' armor. The rivals were Ajax and Odysseus, and the issue was decided by a vote on which man had done more for the Greek cause. Odysseus was adjudged the winner, but Ajax questioned the fairness of the decision. In a rage, he set out to murder his fellow chieftains. Athena caused him to go mad, so that he fell upon the sheep and cattle that had been taken as spoils, instead of upon the chieftains. When Ajax recovered sanity, so deep was his humiliation that he took his own life.

Helenus, son of Priam, and a prophet, was captured; he told the Greeks that Troy could fall only to the bow and arrows of Heracles, wielded by Philoctetes, and to the assault of Neoptolemus (who is also called Pyrrhus), son of Achilles by Deidamia, daughter of King Lycomedes of Scyros. The union of Achilles and Deidamia was either at the time when Achilles was in hiding there, or when he later captured Scyros as an incidental exploit during the siege of Troy. Neoptolemus came most willingly, and was given his father's armor. But Philoctetes, after his ten years of pain and lonely exile on Lemnos, was embittered against the Greek army, and could only with difficulty be prevailed upon. The most familiar story of how he was won over is that Odysseus and Neoptolemus, sent to fetch him, tried to trick him into believing that Neoptolemus was also at odds with the Greek army and would take him home. But just when the trick had succeeded, Neoptolemus found himself morally unable to continue the deception; he was on the point of actually taking Philoctetes home when Heracles intervened and commanded Philoctetes to go to Troy. Philoctetes acceded, and his wound was healed by Podalirius. Among the victims of the fierce young Neoptolemus was Eurypylus, son of Telephus.

The fall. Odysseus and Diomedes entered Troy in disguise and stole the Palladium, an image of Athena that protected the city as long as it remained there. But even now, doomed though it was, the city did not fall. Finally the Greeks entered upon an elaborate scheme of deception. A great wooden horse was built, the chief carpenter being a minor hero named Epeus. The mightiest of the Greek warriors hid in the belly of the horse, as it stood on the beach, while the rest of the host sailed away as if for home. Really they only withdrew behind the nearby island of Tenedos. While the Trojans were wondering at the strange object, an apparent deserter was brought in. He told a plausible story: that his name was Sinon, that he had stayed behind to escape the Greeks, fearing that they would kill him as they had his chief, Palamedes; the horse had been built as an offering to Athena, to atone for the theft of the Palladium; its great size was intended to prevent the Trojans from taking it into the city, because if it entered Troy it would have the same protective power that the Palladium had had. Most of the Trojans were convinced, but Laocoon, priest of Poseidon, warned them to beware of a trick. Even as he spoke, two great serpents swam in from the sea, seized Laocoon and his two sons, and killed them. Convinced that Laocoon had been punished by the gods for bad counsel, the Trojans now dragged the horse into the city, knocking down part of the wall to do so. In reality, the serpents were sent by Poseidon, who was intent on Troy's destruction and feared that the Trojans would heed Laocoon. (Throughout the war, many of the gods took sides. Hera, Athena, and Poseidon favored the Greeks; Apollo, Ares, and Artemis, the Trojans. Zeus was generally neutral.) Cassandra, too, warned of the trick but was disregarded, as always. It is sometimes said that Helen walked about the wooden horse and called to the men inside, imitating their wives' voices; but Odysseus restrained his fellows from answering and they remained concealed.

Troy now fell. By night the men descended from the horse, the fleet was recalled by a signal, and a period of slaughter and rapine ensued, with Neoptolemus the leader of the assault. Neoptolemus killed old Priam while he was sitting at an altar; Astyanax, Hector's infant son, was thrown to his death from the wall; Polyxena, daughter of Priam, was sacrificed at the grave of Achilles; Cassandra was raped at the altar of Athena by the Locrian Ajax; under the strain of such suffering, Hecuba went mad, and was transformed into a hell-hound. Only two prominent Trojans escaped, Antenor and Aeneas. Aeneas, his aged father Anchises on his shoulders, his son Ascanius at his side, and a small group of followers in attendance, made his way from the burning city. His wife, Creusa, was lost in the turmoil and smoke of the city's destruction. Menelaus killed Deiphobus, son of Priam, who, after Paris's death, had become the husband of Helen. (Paris had died a little before, by an arrow shot by Philoctetes. He had gone back to Oenone on Mount Ida; when Oenone, who was skilled in medicinal herbs, would not heal him, he returned to Troy to die.) Menelaus meant to kill Helen too, but as soon as he beheld her beauty once more, he forgave her. The surviving Trojan women were taken as slaves; Cassandra became the concubine of Agamemnon, Andromache the slave of Neoptolemus.

The returns. The final chapter of the story of Troy concerns the return home of the Greek heroes. The fleet became scattered, and various difficulties were encountered. Some of the Greeks, however, reached home without serious hazard: old Nestor to Pylos, Idomeneus to Crete, Diomedes to Aetolia, and Philoctetes to Thessaly, though there are accounts of how both Diomedes (in sorrow at the infidelity of his wife, Aegialia) and Philoctetes again set out from home and founded cities in south Italy. Neoptolemus went to Epirus, and later back to the area of south Thessaly from which Achilles had come. Menelaus was blown completely off his course and wound up in Egypt. Here, according to one deviationist account, he found Helen, who had really been in Egypt (where Paris had unknowingly left her during a stop there on his way back to Troy) all through the war; at Troy there had been only a phantom of Helen, over which the ten years of battle had taken place. In any event, Menelaus and Helen returned to Sparta and lived there happily, eventually being transported to eternal bliss in the Elysian Fields. The Locrian Ajax was killed on his way home by Athena and Poseidon, in punishment for his rape of Cassandra.

The two most celebrated returns are those of Agamemnon, which is told under **Atreus,** and **Odysseus.**

Literature, both ancient and modern, on the Trojan story is of course abundant. Apart from the *Iliad* and the *Aeneid* (Book 2 has the best description of the fall of Troy) there are several plays based on incidents of the war: Sophocles' *Ajax* and *Philoctetes,* Euripides' *Iphigenia at Aulis, Iphigenia in Tauris, Hecuba,* and *The Trojan Women.* Seneca, too, wrote a *Trojan Women.* Among nineteenth- and twentieth-century works on Trojan themes may be mentioned Wordsworth's *Laodamia* (1814), Tennyson's *Oenone* (1842), George Meredith's *Cassandra* (1862), Lord de Tabley's *Philoctetes* (1866), William Morris's *The Death of Paris* (in *The Earthly Paradise,* 1868–1870), D. G. Rossetti's *Troy Town* (1870), John Masefield's *Tale of Troy* (1932), and Archibald MacLeish's *The Trojan Horse* (1952). The story of Troilus and Cressida appears, above all, in the famous versions of Chaucer and Shakespeare.

Turnus (tur′nus) was the principal antagonist of **Aeneas** in Italy.

Tyche (tī′kē) is the personification of luck.

Tydeus (tī′dūs) was one of the Seven against **Thebes.**

Tyndareus (tin-dar'ē-us) was the husband of **Leda.**

Typhoeus (tī-fō'ūs), or **Typhon** (tī'fon), or **Typhaon** (tī-fā'on), the most monstrous of giants, attacked **Zeus.**

Tyro (tī'rō) was the daughter of **Salmoneus.**

Ulysses (ū-lis'ēz) is the Roman form of **Odysseus.**

Urania (ū-rā'ni-a) was one of the nine **Muses,** patroness of astronomy.

Uranus (ū'ra-nus) is Father Sky. See **Earth and Sky.**

Venus (vē'nus) is the Roman name of **Aphrodite.**

Vertumnus (ver-tum'nus) was the Roman god of change (the name is connected with Latin *vertere*, to turn), and was chiefly connected with the changes of the seasons. Vertumnus was in love with Pomona, the goddess of agricultural fruitfulness, but wooed her without success, until he changed himself into the form of an old women. In this guise he so successfully sang the praises of both himself and Pomona, and so winningly portrayed them as an ideal couple that when he changed back to his own form he easily prevailed on
* Pomona to accept him.

Vesper (ves'per) is the evening star.

Vesta (ves'ta) is the Roman name of **Hestia.**

Vulcan (vul'kan) is the Roman name of **Hephaestus.**

Wind Deities. The winds are kept by King Aeolus, son of Hippotas, in the island of Aeolia. The principal winds are Boreas, or Aquilo, the north wind; Zephyrus, or Favonius, the west wind; Notus, or Auster, the south wind; and Eurus, the east wind. Only Boreas and Zephyrus are commonly personified. For the story of how Boreas swept Orithyia away and by her became father of Zetes and Calais, see under **Athens.**

Xanthus (zan'thus) is a river near Troy.

Zephyrus (zef'i-rus) is the west wind. See **Wind Deities.**

*add: The story is told by Ovid, *Metamorphoses*, 14.

Zethus (zē′thus), son of Zeus and Antiope, was ruler of **Thebes.**

Zeus (zūs), whom the Romans called Jupiter, is originally the god of the sky; the root of his name in both Greek and Latin means "bright." He is god of storms as well as of the clear sky, and his most constant attribute in ancient art is the biconical thunderbolt which he carries. He is also the ruler of the *
gods, the "father of gods and men" in Homer, Virgil, and other authors; in this role he is the protector of earthly kings, and of strangers and suppliants as well. He is a figure of majesty, mature, bearded, often carrying a scepter, sometimes enthroned; he may be accompanied by his sacred bird, the eagle, and may be wearing on his breast or over his left arm the aegis, the fringed cloaklike protective covering of magic invulnerability (in origin simply the goatskin cloak of the shepherd) which is often worn also by his daughter Athena. The classic description of him is in the first book of the *Iliad*, where we are told that his "ambrosial locks flow down from his immortal head," and his very nod "shakes great Olympus."

This august and paternal figure, wielder of scepter and thunderbolt, is only one part of Zeus. It is the picture that begins in the Homeric poems, is prevalent in Greek tragedy, is adopted by Virgil, and descends to most subsequent literature that touches on myth. And yet, though the sky figure and ruler are the basic ingredients and are never quite lost sight of, the more intimate and manlike aspects of Zeus are conspicuous in myth. Zeus rules the gods less as an absolute monarch than as the somewhat uneasy *paterfamilias* of the obstreperous and independent Olympian family. He is the spouse of a jealous and outspoken queen, Hera. By her, and by other divine consorts, he is the father of many of the best-known deities. The role in which he is most familiar in myth is the least august of all, as the principal in a long and brilliant succession of amorous adventures with mortal beauties, which he engages in while he tries, usually unsuccessfully, to elude the watchful eye of Hera, and by which he becomes the father of many of the most distinguished heroes of mythology.

In this picture of Zeus, though we are made dimly aware that there were divine rulers before him, there is little thought of evolution, growth, or change, and the picture is essentially stationary and continuous. But there is another aspect of Zeus, which might be called the Hesiodic picture, because it is derived largely from Hesiod's *Theogony*. In this other picture Zeus is born, achieves by struggle his power and his character as divine ruler, even dies in some stories. It is possible that some elements of this other Zeus go back to the religion and the stories of the Minoan civilization that had its center in Crete and was flourishing in the Aegean when the people whom we call the Greeks entered this area in the second millennium B.C. The story of Zeus's birth, at any rate, is associated with Crete. Cronus, warned that he would be overthrown as divine ruler by his son, swallowed his children as they were born. But his wife Rhea hid her latest born, Zeus, in a cave on Mount Ida (or Mount Dicte) in Crete, and gave her ravenous spouse a stone

*read: (keraunos), his weapon of destruction. He is also the ruler of

wrapped in swaddling clothes to swallow. The baby was nursed by a she-goat, Amalthea, and his crying was drowned out by young warriors called Curetes, who sang and clashed their shields. Zeus grew to maturity, rebelled against his father, and defeated him and his fellow Titans in a furious ten-year struggle. He was supported in the rebellion by his five brothers and sisters, Hestia, Demeter, Hera, Hades, and Poseidon (who had been regurgitated by Cronus, either when he tried to swallow the stone substituted for Zeus, or later, when Metis, who was to be Zeus's first wife, administered an emetic); by children of Earth and Sky other than the Titans, namely the Cyclopes and the Hecatoncheires ("hundred-handed ones"), both groups having been freed (by Zeus) from Tartarus, where Cronus had imprisoned them; by the river Styx and her children; and by Promētheus, though he was the son of a Titan, Iapetus. At last the thunderbolt of Zeus prevailed, and the Titans were relegated to Tartarus, all except Atlas, brother of Prometheus, who was assigned to support the sky on his shoulders. The Hecatoncheires were made their warders.

Next came the most famous of Zeus's struggles, that with **Prometheus.**

Finally, Zeus had to overcome the onset, in three separate waves, of the Giants, who are usually represented as offspring of Earth and as being urged by her to attack the Olympians. The first battle, the Gigantomachy ("fight with the Giants") proper, consisted of a general onslaught of all the Giants, a boisterous group of huge, snake-legged creatures. The battle took place on the plains of Phlegra, situated perhaps in Thessaly. It ended in the defeat and imprisonment of the Giants. Enceladus writhes under Sicily, which Athena threw at him. His presence there is still manifested by the eruptions of Mount Etna. Others of the defeated Giants were Porphyrion and Alcyoneus. Next came Typhoeus, or Typhon, another son of Earth (though Hesiod calls him son of Hera), a prodigious monster with a hundred hissing, fire-breathing heads. He, too, was humbled by the thunderbolt and languishes in Tartarus. The third attack was by Otus and Ephialtes, the Aloadae, giant sons of Poseidon by Iphimedea, wife of Aloeus (hence the name Aloadae). These brothers performed an infamous feat of strength and insolence; they piled Mount Ossa on Mount Olympus, and Mount Pelion on Ossa (they are the highest mountains of Thessaly) in order to reach heaven and attack the gods. They were destroyed by Zeus in the attempt.

Turning back now to the Homeric picture of Zeus, we can distinguish two areas of interest, Zeus as ruler, and Zeus as husband and lover. Zeus as ruler, though of continuing importance in myth, is a relatively colorless figure of whom little need be said. The usual tradition is that, after the overthrow of Cronus, Zeus and his two brothers, Poseidon and Hades, cast lots in order to divide the rule of the universe. In the lot Zeus got dominion over the sky, Poseidon over the sea, and Hades over the underworld. (It had been agreed among them that the earth and Mount Olympus were to be common ground.) Poseidon and Hades have, as a rule, undisputed authority over their own territories, but Zeus is the supreme power.

The usual depiction of Zeus's marital and amorous life has him married to Hera and engaging in a long series of infidelities with goddesses and mortal women. But there is in Hesiod a succession of six divine wives preceding Hera. A serious intent is clearly present in Hesiod's account, a desire to relate to the divine ruler certain concepts and figures which are important in the poet's systematization of religious thought. The first of these divine wives or consorts is Metis ("Wisdom"). She was destined, had she survived, to bear first Athena and then a son who would overthrow Zeus. Zeus swallowed her while she was pregnant with Athena, who later sprang fully armed from her father's forehead. Second was Themis, a Titaness, who gave birth to the Horae ("Seasons") and the Fates. Third was the ocean nymph Eurynome, mother of the three Graces, or **Charites. Demeter,** Zeus's sister, mother of Persephone, was fourth. Fifth was Mnemosyne ("Memory"), who was, appropriately enough, mother of the nine **Muses.** Sixth, and last before Hera, was Leto, mother of Apollo and Artemis. For the seventh and principal wife, see **Hera.** Dione, who is virtually unknown in mythology, is said by Homer to have been a wife of Zeus and by him mother of Aphrodite. Still another divine consort was Maia, daughter of Atlas and mother of Hermes.

The offspring of these divine mates of Zeus are all deities, whether prominent or insignificant. As a rule, the fruit of Zeus's love affairs with mortal women are mortal men, and they include many of the great heroes of Greek myth, among them Perseus, son of Zeus and Danae, and Heracles, son of Zeus and Alcmena. These earthly adventures of Zeus are closely linked with stories concerning the heroic offspring, and are therefore described elsewhere. Here it need be said only that among them are some of the most familiar incidents in which Zeus appears.

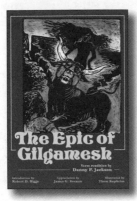

The Epic of Gilgamesh
2nd Edition

Verse rendition by Danny P. Jackson
Introduction by Robert D. Biggs
Illustrations by Thom Kapheim
Interpretive essay by James G. Keenan

B&W illustrations, 115 pp. (1997, Reprint 2000)
Standard Paperback Edition, ISBN 978-0-86516-352-2

Reanimates the story of Gilgamesh and Enkidu for modern readers, bringing it new life through indelible poetic images

Though *The Epic of Gilgamesh* exists in several editions, this version has been undertaken with a very specific intent—to remain faithful to the source material while attempting to convey the poetic scope of a work that is both lusty and tender and that retains the ability to arouse compassion and empathy in all who follow Gilgamesh on his journey. The total is a new edition that delights, informs, and stimulates readers to a new appreciation of this age-old tale.

Includes: Story Commentary • Historical Notes • Illustrated Introduction • 15 Original Woodcut Prints • 18 Photos

---

The Essential Euripides: *Dancing in Dark Times*
Robert Emmet Meagher

xii + 556 pp. (2001) Paperback, ISBN: 978-0-86516-513-7

Additional titles translated by Robert Emmet Maegher
Euripides *Bakkhai*

vi + 97 pp. (1995) Paperback, ISBN 978-0-86516-285-3

Aeschylus: *Seven Against Thebes*

x + 44 pp. (1996) Paperback, ISBN 978-0-86516-337-9

Euripides: *Hekabe*

vii + 55 pp. (1995) Paperback, ISBN 978-0-86516-330-0

Euripides: *Iphigenia at Aulis and Iphigenia in Tauris*

176 pp. (1993) Hardbound, ISBN 978-0-86516-266-2

BOLCHAZY-CARDUCCI PUBLISHERS, INC.
WWW.BOLCHAZY.COM